The Essential Guide
to LibreOffice

Published by Agora Business Publications LLP

Agora Business Publications LLP
Nesfield House
Broughton Hall Business Park
Skipton
BD23 3AN

Publisher: Victoria Burrill
Author: Simon Fraser

Phone: 01756 693 180
Fax: 01756 693 196
Email: cs@agorapublications.co.uk
Web: www.agorabusinesspublications.co.uk

ISBN: 978-1-908245-07-6

Agora Business Publications LLP. Nesfield House, Broughton Hall Business Park, Skipton Yorkshire, BD23 3AN.
Registered in England No. OC323533, VAT No. GB 893 3184 95.

Table of Contents

Introduction to LibreOffice: the Leading, Free, Office Productivity Suite

Dear Reader,

More and more users are becoming fed up of paying for something that they can get for nothing. LibreOffice is the leading alternative to Microsoft Office and as the name may suggest, it is completely free.

LibreOffice is a suite of office applications that have been designed from the ground-up to provide a consistent, simple-to-use interface with a familiar look and feel.

LibreOffice is compatible with most popular office suites, so you don't need to worry about having trouble when sending documents to friends or colleagues using other systems. Furthermore, LibreOffice can be run on all of today's principal operating systems.

LibreOffice is free software, but this gives you more than just money in the bank. Software that is open-source allows independent security experts to thoroughly test and verify the applications provided, allowing you to be confident that you're not opening a hole in your computer's defences.

Once you've decided that LibreOffice is the way forward, you will want to read this book; turning yourself into an expert user as you uncover the professional's secrets. Read on to discover tips and tricks that will save you time and energy, enabling you to quickly and easily produce documents of the highest quality.

Best wishes,

Simon Fraser

Simon Fraser
Author, *The Essential Guide to LibreOffice*
and Editor-in-Chief of RUN LINUX!

PART 1

Quick and Easy Installation of LibreOffice

The first step in becoming an expert user of LibreOffice is to get the suite installed. This is a simple process and should take no longer than a few minutes.

LibreOffice is open source software which means that anybody can view the source code and use it to build an application. This allows LibreOffice to be installed on virtually all operating systems currently available. Don't worry though, you won't need to build the application yourself. For the majority of popular operating systems, LibreOffice has been pre-built and handy installers have already been created. You can use one of these installers to get LibreOffice up and running on your computer.

In the following chapters, I will show you in detail how to install LibreOffice on PCs running both the Windows and Ubuntu operating systems. I will then discuss what to do if you want to use LibreOffice on a different operating system.

Regardless of your platform, the installation of LibreOffice is easy and the tips and tricks contained in the remainder of this book will allow you to create professional-looking documents in no time.

1. Installation on Windows

LibreOffice provides binary set-up files that can be downloaded for free from their website. To download and install LibreOffice, simply do the following:

1. Open a web browser such as Internet Explorer or Firefox and go to: www.libreoffice.org/download.

2. Select **Main Installer** as shown below.

Download the software

3. Select **Open** or **Run** (depending upon your browser) from the pop-up dialog.

4. The installation program will now be downloaded to your computer and this may take a few minutes depending upon the speed of your connection.

5. A dialog introducing the installation will appear. Select **Next** to proceed.

6. Enter your name and organisation (leave blank if not needed), and select **Next**.

7. The installation is now ready; select **Install**.

8. If you're using a recent version of Windows, you may now be asked to confirm whether to allow the installation of LibreOffice. You should select **Yes** or **Continue** – depending upon the particular version used.

9. After a few minutes the installation will complete; select **Finish** and you are ready to start using LibreOffice.

Although it's not strictly necessary, you can now install the built-in LibreOffice help system by returning to your browser, selecting **LibreOffice built-in help**, and installing in the same way.

2. Installation on Ubuntu

LibreOffice is the default office suite provided with Ubuntu from the 11.04 release onwards. If are you using the latest version of Ubuntu, you may find that LibreOffice is already installed.

Check Whether LibreOffice is Already Installed

Obviously there is no need to reinstall LibreOffice if it's already on your computer. To check whether LibreOffice is installed, do the following:

1. Open the Ubuntu Software Centre by selecting the **Ubuntu Software Centre** from the launcher.

2. Enter **LibreOffice** in the search box and press **Enter**.

3. If you see entries for LibreOffice decorated with a green tick as shown below, then LibreOffice is already installed and you can get straight on to using it.

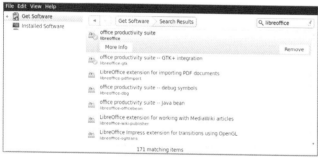

Green ticks show LibreOffice is installed

Uninstall OpenOffice

If you discover that you need to install LibreOffice then it will be necessary first to uninstall any installations of its predecessor OpenOffice. You will need to do this as they are essentially the same application, and having both suites installed could cause some conflicts between the two. To uninstall OpenOffice, do the following:

1. Open the Ubuntu Software Centre by selecting **Applications** > **Ubuntu Software Centre**.

2. Enter **OpenOffice** in the search box and press **Enter**.

3. If OpenOffice is installed you will now see several OpenOffice entries decorated with a green tick.

Green ticks show OpenOffice is installed

4. Select each entry and then click **Remove**.

5. You may be prompted to enter your password to provide the privileges necessary to remove the software.

6. When all of the OpenOffice entries no longer have a green tick then OpenOffice has been successfully uninstalled.

Install LibreOffice from the Ubuntu Software Centre

You can now proceed with the installation of LibreOffice. While it is possible to download LibreOffice for Ubuntu from the website, installing from the Ubuntu Software Centre will ensure that you have immediate access to any changes making it much easier to keep your software up-to-date. To install using the Ubuntu Software Centre, do the following:

1. Open the Ubuntu Software Centre by selecting **Applications > Ubuntu Software Centre**.

2. Enter **LibreOffice** in the search box and press **Enter**.

3. If you see no entries, proceed to step **4**, otherwise skip to step **12**.

4. Select **Edit > Software Sources**.

5. At this point (and a few others) you may be prompted to enter your password to provide the privileges necessary to remove the software. This is normal and your password should be entered.

6. Select the **Other Software** tab.

7. Select **Add**.

8. Enter **ppa:libreoffice/ppa** and select **Add Source**.

9. Your list of sources should now resemble the screenshot shown below.

Software sources

10. Select **Close**.

11. The list of available packages will be updated. After a few seconds (depending upon the speed of your Internet connection) the list of available packages will be populated and look something like this:

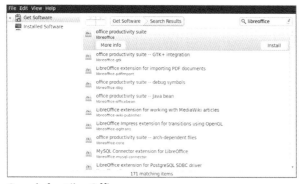

Search for LibreOffice

12. Locate the entry titled **Office productivity suite** and select **Install**. This installs the core LibreOffice suite.

13. Enter **LibreOffice-Gnome** in the search box and press **Enter**.

14. Locate the entry title **Office productivity suite – GNOME integration** and select **Install**. This installs some extra tools to make LibreOffice work better with your desktop.

15. Select **In Progress** from the left-hand-side of the Ubuntu Software Centre.

16. You will see a screen, similar to the next screenshot that shows the progress of the installation. When both package installations have reached 100%, LibreOffice will be fully installed and you will be ready to get going.

Installation in progress

Once you have LibreOffice installed in Ubuntu, it will be kept up-to-date during the course of applying system security updates. If, however, you want to be sure that you have the latest version, you can quickly update it manually. Simply open a terminal and type **sudo apt-get update; apt-get install libreoffice**

3. Installation on Other Operating Systems

As LibreOffice is open source software you should be able to install it on practically any operating system. Installers for Mac OS X, Red Hat-based Linux distributions (rpm) and Debian-based Linux distributions (deb) are available for download at: www.libreoffice.org/download/.

When downloading an rpm or deb file for Linux, you will need to know what your hardware platform is in order to choose a file to download; as when you choose an operating system on the download page you will have to decide whether you want the 32 bit or 64 bit version of the installer (referred to as **x86** and **x64** respectively).

To determine which version you want, open a terminal window and type **uname –i** This will give you the hardware platform of the current machine.

Determine the hardware platform

If you have a hardware platform of the form **i386**, **i686** or something similar you will need the **x86** version of the downloader. If you get a value of the form **x86_64** then you will need the **x64** version of the installer.

Once downloaded, the installation process is much the same as the ones for Windows and Ubuntu which are described above.

If you are feeling adventurous or you are using an operating system that we haven't mentioned then you can actually create your own LibreOffice installer from the source code which you can download from the site above.

PART 2

Get Up and Running
with LibreOffice

Now you have LibreOffice installed, it's time to get using it. The tagline of LibreOffice is 'The Productivity Suite', and you will soon see how using it can save you time and energy. In Part 2, I'll show you how to get the best out of LibreOffice's key tools.

Although there are actually six tools included within the LibreOffice toolset, we will concentrate on the four principal applications: Writer, Calc, Impress and Base. These are the tools that actually get used in practice and, while the other programs can be useful, they tend to be fairly limited in their application. You'll also discover how to ensure that others can read your documents, by converting your creations into Microsoft Office and PDF formats.

I'm not going to patronise you by explaining how to open a document and make some text bold; instead, you'll learn how to save time and make your documents look like they've been produced by a professional.

Throughout Part 2, we'll cover each of the four LibreOffice tools in detail, enabling you to get the most out of the application with very little effort. From navigating quickly within your document, and performing actions quickly using keyboard shortcuts, to achieving that professional look and feel, Part 2 aims to get you up and running in no time!

4. A Quick Introduction to the Tools

The LibreOffice Productivity Suite is a collection of tools designed to meet all of your office needs. A common interface is used so that once you have become adept at using one tool, it should be easy to learn to use the others. The four principle components of LibreOffice are **Writer**, **Calc**, **Impress** and **Base**. Other components include **Draw** – a diagram and drawing tool capable of creating all sorts of graphics from sketches to complex 3D illustrations – and **Math** – an equation editor that enables you to format equations quickly and easily in a way that allows them to be seamlessly integrated into your documents.

Word Processing with Writer

Writer is LibreOffice's text editor. Writer is equally capable of producing a shopping list and a novel. It has many of the same features as other popular word processors, but also has a selection of unique tools that you are sure to find invaluable. Anyone who has previously used another word processor will find Writer quick and easy to use thanks to its familiar user interface and intuitive design.

The Writer interface

Spreadsheets with Calc

Calc is LibreOffice's spreadsheet program and can be used for much the same variety of applications as the leading proprietary spreadsheet tools. A full suite of functions make creating formulas simple, and the formula builder ensures that this remains easy even when performing complex calculations. Calc also enables you to use charts to visualise complex data and provides analysis tools to assist you in making conclusions based upon that data.

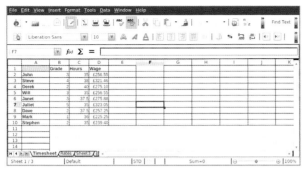

The Calc interface

Presentations with Impress

Impress is the LibreOffice application that allows you to make professional-standard presentations. Impress is an advanced tool that incorporates special effects, sound and audio into your presentations to ensure that your audience will both understand, and be entertained by, what you have to say.

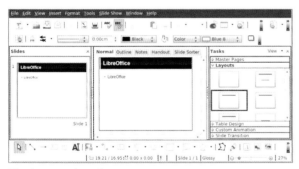

The Impress interface

Data Management with Base

Base is a data management tool that can be used to interface to existing databases or create new ones from scratch. A wide-range of database technologies can be used under the hood, ensuring that you will be able to use other database tools in tandem with Base and manage your data effectively and efficiently.

The Base interface

Ensuring Your Document is Saved the Right Way

One of the concerns you may have when starting to use LibreOffice is that you may think that you'll need anybody you work with to install LibreOffice too. Not only is this not the case, but LibreOffice will allow you to save your document in a multitude of formats enabling you to work effectively with anybody using any of the more popular office tools. In addition, LibreOffice can also export your documents to the portable document format (PDF) that will allow anybody to read your documents regardless of whether they have a word processor at all.

Save Your Document in Microsoft Office Format

One of the most common office formats that LibreOffice provides support for is Microsoft Office. To use a LibreOffice tool to save a document in the Microsoft Office format, do the following:

1. Select **File > Save As…**

2. Choose the correct format for your version of Microsoft Office from the **Save as type** drop-down list.

This example demonstrates saving a Writer document, but these steps can be applied just as easily to Calc and Impress documents.

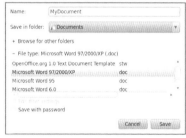

Choosing the file type

3. Select **Save** and your document will be saved in the correct format.

As well as saving your document, LibreOffice is also able to open documents in these formats so there will be no need to keep converting to Microsoft Office format on subsequent saves.

Export Your Document as a PDF File

In order to save a LibreOffice document as a PDF, do the following:

1. Select **File > Export as PDF**.

2. Select **Export**.

3. Choose where to save the PDF file and select **Save**.

When you export a document as a PDF, LibreOffice will not change the format of the document you have open. Therefore, if you want to save a later version of a document as a PDF, you will need to explicitly export it again.

Get a Jump Start to Using LibreOffice

As with many office suites, LibreOffice can be driven with both the mouse and the keyboard. Professionals will tell you that once you have gained a basic familiarity with a tool, using the keyboard to drive an application gives you a significant advantage. Not only is it much quicker to use than the mouse, but using the mouse requires a level of precision that research has shown surprisingly few people possess. For the best experience it is recommended that you try to use keyboard shortcuts as soon as you start using a tool as the sooner you begin using them, the more familiar they will feel. After a short while you will wonder how anyone can bare the drudgery of using the mouse.

Understanding Keyboard Focus

In order to use the keyboard to drive an application successfully, it is important to understand the concept of keyboard focus. Keyboard focus determines what button, checkbox or menu on the screen will respond when you press keys on the keyboard. You can see which element has focus as it will look slightly different to other elements of the same type. The exact difference depends upon the operating system being used. The next image shows the difference between focused and non-focused buttons in Windows and Linux. In each case the **OK** button has the focus.

LibreOffice buttons

A list of some of the keyboard shortcuts that can be used in conjunction with keyboard focus, and throughout LibreOffice is presented in the table below:

Key combination	Effect
⏎ Enter	Activates a button that is currently focused.
Space	Toggles the value of a focused checkbox.
Esc	Closes a dialog box or cancels an action.
↑	Scrolls up a focused list.
↓	Scrolls down a focused list.
Alt + ↓	Opens a focused drop-down list.
Tab	Moves the focus to the next element in a dialog.
⇧ Shift + Tab	Moves the focus to the previous element in a dialog.

General Keyboard Shortcuts

A list of some of the more useful keyboards shortcuts that can be used in all the LibreOffice tools is presented in the table below:

Key combination	Effect
Delete	Deletes the selected item.
Ctrl + M	Removes all formatting from the selected item.
Ctrl + N	Creates a document.
Ctrl + O	Opens a document.
Ctrl + S	Saves the current document.
Ctrl + P	Prints the current document.
Ctrl + Q	Quits the current application.
Ctrl + X	Cut – removes the currently selected item and places it on the clipboard.
Ctrl + C	Copies the currently selected item to the clipboard.
Ctrl + V	Pastes the item that is currently on the clipboard to the document.
Ctrl + A	Selects the document's entire contents.
Ctrl + Z	Will undo the last action.
Ctrl + Y	Will redo the last action that was undone.
Ctrl + Y + ⇧ Shift	Repeats the last action.
Ctrl + F	Opens the **Find** & **Replace** dialog.
Ctrl + F + ⇧ Shift	Searches again for the text that was last searched for.

Key combination	Effect
Ctrl + I	Makes the text of the currently selected item *italic*.
Ctrl + B	Makes the text of the currently selected item **bold**.
Ctrl + U	Makes the text of the currently selected item <u>underlined</u>.

Using Draw to Edit PDFs

Although I have said that I would not be describing LibreOffice's draw tool, there is one application of this tool that is too useful to omit: Draw gives you the capability to open, edit and save PDFs – a functionality that can only usually be found in expensive, proprietary tools. To edit a PDF with Draw, simply do the following:

1. Select **File > Open** and locate the PDF file that you wish to edit.

2. Double-click on a piece of text that you wish to change, and make the alteration.

3. Repeat the process until you have made all of the required changes. You can also make changes to the positioning of items and add new graphical features using Draw's standard functionality.

4. When you have finished your changes, don't save the document. Instead, select **File > Export as PDF...**

5. Select **Export**.

6. Choose a location to save the altered PDF and select **Save**.

The results are not always perfect, but for making small changes Draw has everything you need.

5. Produce High-quality Documents Efficiently with Writer

Navigate Through Your Document Quickly and Easily

When you have a large document, you can often find yourself continually scrolling up and down trying to find a specific piece of text. Writer provides a more effective way of getting around your document that allows you to quickly find and move to a particular section, picture, or table – the navigator. To use the navigator to find a given section do the following:

1. Select **View** > **Navigator** to open the navigator.

2. Open the **Headings** to see a list of all level 1 headings.

3. Drill down into the appropriate heading until you find the heading of the section you require.

4. Double-click on that heading and the document will be moved to the appropriate section. For example, to get to the **Process** section in the navigator shown below, you would click the **plus** next to **Headings**, then **Design**, and finally double-click on **Process**.

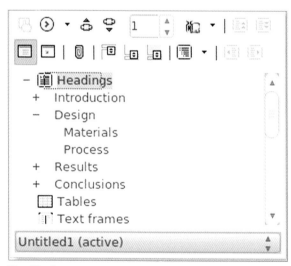

The Navigator

If there are parts of your document which you will need to return frequently, you can add bookmarks to your document and use the navigator to browse between them. To add a bookmark and then use the navigator to return to it, do the following:

1. Go to the commonly used location in your document.

2. Select **Insert > Bookmark**.

3. Enter a memorable name for the bookmark and select **OK**. The bookmark is created and you are returned to the document.

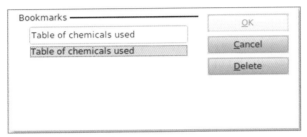

Entering a bookmark

4. When you wish to return to the location of the bookmark, open the navigator by pressing **F5**, and then open the **Bookmarks**, find the appropriate bookmark and double-click on it.

To dock the navigator to the left-hand-side of the Writer window press the **Ctrl** key and double-click on a grey part of the window. The navigator can be undocked in the same way.

Switch Between Styles Instantly

Typically, the formatting bar is used to make formatting changes to your document. However, as you will generally be using the keyboard to write your document, this can really interrupt your flow. It has been shown that using the keyboard alone can be three times faster than having to keep switching to the mouse.

The following table contains keyboard shortcuts that allow you to change paragraphs to the most common styles:

Key combination	Effect
Ctrl + 1 End	Applies the **Heading 1** style.
Ctrl + 2 ↓	Applies the **Heading 2** style.
Ctrl + 3 Pg Dn	Applies the **Heading 3** style.
Ctrl + 4 ←	Applies the **Heading 4** style.
Ctrl + 0 Ins	Applies the **Text Body** style. Akin to removing all existing formatting.

In addition, many of the other functions of the formatting bar can be replicated with keyboard shortcuts. Some have been described previously, but the following table describes shortcuts that are specific to Writer:

Key combination	Effect
Ctrl + E	Centres the text.
Ctrl + J	Justifies the text.
Ctrl + L	Left-aligns the text.
Ctrl + R	Right-aligns the text.
Ctrl + D	Double underlines the current selection.
Ctrl + ⇧ Shift + P	Makes the current selection superscript.
Ctrl + ⇧ Shift + B	Makes the current selection subscript.

Automatically Correct Your Most Common Typing Errors

When you try and type **recieve** into Writer you will find that it will automatically correct the spelling mistake. Mistakes such as these are corrected by default, but you can extend the functionality so that it works best for you. If, for example, you know that you have trouble spelling **accommodation** you can add the common misspellings to the list of auto-corrections. To add to the list of auto-corrections, do the following:

1. Select **Tools > AutoCorrect Options**.

2. Enter the misspelling in the **Replace** field – here this may be **acommodation**.

3. Enter the correct spelling in the **With** field. In this instance, this would be **accommodation**, as shown.

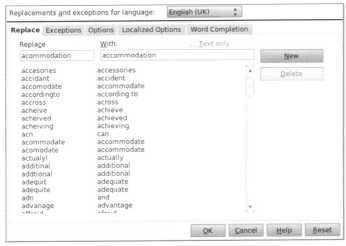

Adding an auto-correction

4. Select **New** and then **OK**.

5. If you now type your misspelling you will see that it is automatically corrected by Writer.

You can use AutoCorrect for more than just spelling mistakes. If you work for a company called **Johnsons Writing and Spelling Company Limited**, you may get fed up writing the company name all the time. You can create an auto-correction that replaces **jws** with the full name and save yourself a great deal of time.

If you want to deliberately misspell a word without turning off the automatic correction, spell the word correctly and press space or enter a punctuation mark, then use the arrow keys to move the cursor back into the word and change the required letters before moving the cursor back to the end of the line.

Give Your Document Clarity with Quick Visual Separation

Horizontal lines are often a good way to break up a long document. However, when you try and insert them, it can often be difficult to get them to fit the page, and you spend ages trying to get the line exactly the right size. Writer provides some shortcuts to produce the perfect horizontal line in just a few key presses. Move the cursor to where you want to place a line, and then select a shortcut from the following table. In each instance you need to press a key three times and then the **Enter** key. Unlike a normal keyboard shortcut, you will see the characters as you press the keys, but don't worry they will disappear as soon as the line is inserted.

Key combination	Effect
`-` `-` `-` ←Enter	————————————————
`-` `-` `-` ←Enter	————————————————
`*8` `*8` `*8` ←Enter	════════════════
`=` `=` `=` ←Enter	════════════════
`#3` `#3` `#3` ←Enter	════════════════
`~` `~` `~` ←Enter	════════════════

Ensure that All Changes are Clearly Marked

If you ask somebody to review a document you have been writing, you would like them to able to do so in a way that allows you to see what they've changed. Similarly, when a document has multiple authors, you will often need to know who has made what change. In both cases, there will come a point where you need to decide whether the changes made by others are to your liking and whether you wish to incorporate them into your document.

Writer provides a facility for recording the changes made to a document. The content, author and time of the change are recorded and each change can be accepted or rejected as required. In order to start recording changes, and see how they are clearly marked within your document, do the following:

1. You can start to record changes by checking the **Edit > Changes > Record** checkbox.

2. When you return to your document and start to make a change it will be highlighted.

3. When you hover over the change, the details of the change will be shown in a tool tip.

My merit hath my duty strongly knit,
To theeyou I send this written embassage,
To witness duty, not to show my wit:
Duty so Inserted: Simon Fraser - 02/05/2011 15:07
May make seem bare, in wanting words to show it,

Change details

When you are ready to examine the changes to your document and decide whether to keep them, simply complete the following steps:

1. Select **Edit > Changes > Accept or Reject...**

2. The list of changes which have been neither approved nor rejected is shown. An example is shown below.

Accept or reject changes

3. For each outstanding change, select the change and then select **Accept** or **Reject**. Once a change has been accepted it will not be highlighted and it will look like any other piece of text. If a change is rejected, it will be reverted in your document and all references to the change will be removed.

To stop recording future changes, simply uncheck the **Edit** > **Changes** > **Record** checkbox. If you want to record changes without seeing the details of the changes in your document uncheck the **Edit** > **Changes** > **Show** checkbox.

Improve Your Layout with Page Breaks

I have found that I would often like a particular heading or picture to appear at the top of a page, but I'll get it there and then make a change elsewhere in the document and all my hard work would be undone. Fortunately, there is a solution.

Writer allows you to insert page breaks that will guarantee that the next line will start at the top of a page. To insert a page break, do the following:

1. Place the cursor immediately before the item that you would like to appear at the top of a page.

2. Select **Insert** > **Manual Break...**

3. Choose **Page break** from the list below **Type**.

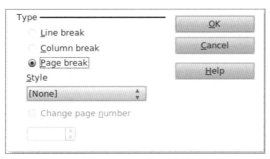

Insert a page break

4. Select **OK** and you will see that a new page has been started before the required item. This will not change regardless of what you do to the preceding text.

Save Time by Defining Your Own Keyboard Shortcuts

While using the built-in keyboard shortcuts can save you a lot of time, using your own keyboard shortcuts can save you even more time. You can define keyboard shortcuts for most actions. Only you will know what actions you perform most often, but I like to define my own keyboard shortcuts for my custom styles and for opening commonly used dialogs such as Paragraph. To create a keyboard shortcut, do the following:

1. Select **Tool > Customize...**

2. Select the **Keyboard** tab.

3. Choose a key combination for your shortcut from the **Shortcut keys list**. If you choose a combination that already has an action assigned, the existing behaviour will be overridden.

4. Select an action to perform in the **Functions** area. To open the **Paragraph** dialog you would choose **Format** from the **Category** list and **Paragraph** from the **Function** list. The screenshot below shows this action being assigned to **Ctrl+T**.

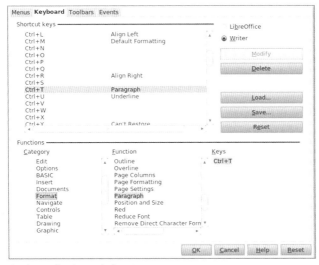

Assign a keyboard shortcut

5. Select **Modify**.

6. Select **OK**. The dialog will close and you will be able to test your new keyboard shortcut.

When you look at the list of keyboard shortcuts you will find many free slots. However, you will need to be aware that keyboard shortcuts can be overridden by your operating system; for example, **F1**, usually means **Help**. Before assigning a keyboard shortcut, therefore, it is well worth trying out your proposed key combination to be sure that it doesn't already do something.

Advanced Searching Using Wild Cards

Sometimes it's useful to search for more than just a recognisable word. Perhaps you've realised that you've had two authors working on a document, and that one has been using -**ise** verb endings and the other -**ize**. Alternatively, you may think that starting a paragraph with **and** is terrible and you'd like to know if this occurs in the document that you are reviewing. Trying to find all of the words that end in -**ize**, -**ized** or -**izing** would be practically impossible with a standard search; as would trying to identify which uses of **and** started a paragraph.

It is possible to search for either of the above examples using Writer's wild card searching. To use wild card searching do the following:

1. Select **Edit** > **Find & Replace**.

2. Select **More Options** to expand the dialog.

3. Check the **Regular expressions** checkbox.

Find with wildcards

4. Enter a wild card search term in the **Search for** box. A list of some of the more useful wild card search terms appears in the following table.

For the **-ize** example, the required search term would be **ize\>|ized\ >|izing\>**

This term could be roughly translated into English as **ize** at the end of a word *or* **ized** at the end of a word *or* **izing** at the end of a word.

To find all the instances of **And** at the start of a paragraph, the required search term would be ^**And**.

Search term	Meaning
|	Match either the term to the left **or** the term to the right.
.	Match any single character.
^	Match the term to the right only at the beginning of a paragraph.
$	Match the term to the left only at the end of a paragraph.
\>	Match the term to the right only at the beginning of a word.
\<	Match the term to the left only at the end of a word.
*	Matches zero or more occurrences of the preceding character.
+	Matches one or more occurrences of the preceding character.

Get Accurate Word Counts

Whether you're writing an essay or an article, there are often times when you need to know the number of words in a document. Whilst it is fairly easy to determine the number of words in the entire document, you rarely want to count every word in the document. Word counts often need to exclude text in tables or footnotes, but this depends entirely upon the circumstances. Unfortunately, Writer cannot offer a solution that will work easily in every situation, but it is always possible – if sometimes a bit fiddly – to get a word count that meets the rules you need. To get a word count for all the text in the main body of the document that contains tables, do the following:

1. Use the mouse or keyboard to select all the text in the body of the document from the start to the first table.

2. Press and hold the **Ctrl** button, while using the mouse or keyboard to select each remaining block of text between tables until you reach the end of the document.

3. Select **Tools > Word Count** to bring up a dialog similar to the one shown in the following screenshot. This will show you the number of words in the selection, which will be the required word count. The total number of words in the document will also be shown as well as the number of characters in the selection and the document.

   Obviously this method could be used to get a word count for any counting method; you would just need to adapt the selection strategy.

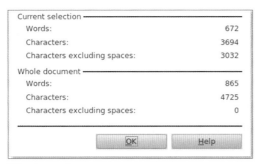

Current selection	
Words:	672
Characters:	3694
Characters excluding spaces:	3032
Whole document	
Words:	865
Characters:	4725
Characters excluding spaces:	0

| OK | Help |

Word count

You can find out more information regarding the contents of your document by selecting **File** > **Properties** and choosing the **Statistics** tab. Here you can quickly find the number of tables, pictures or lines in the document as well as a selection of other details.

Preserve Your Document's History with Versioning

How many times have you been working on a document only to wish that you could refer back to an old version of the text? I commonly decide to rewrite a paragraph or section only to realise a few days later that there was a sentence or two that I'd deleted, but which I wish I hadn't. Even if you don't want to restore old text it can be extremely useful to compare the text in a passage with that from an earlier point in time. This can be particularly true when a document is long-lived and edited over time.

Writer offers the ability to record versions of your document without having to resort to making copies of a file and sticking them in a backup folder. Writer's versioning system allows you to create a historical record of your document that will be maintained in the same file as the document itself. To create and view a version of a document, do the following:

1. Ensure that your file is saved in the LibreOffice ODT format, as versioning cannot be used with non-native file formats.

2. Select **File** > **Versions...**

3. Select **Save New Version**.

4. Enter any comments you have that will enable you to identify the version in the future. For example, you may have something like, **Updated VAT rate to 20% throughout the document**. A little bit of effort in creating a meaningful comment at this stage can prove very useful later when you're trying to find an old version.

5. Select **OK** and you will see the new version in the list of versions as shown below. Select **Close** to close the dialog.

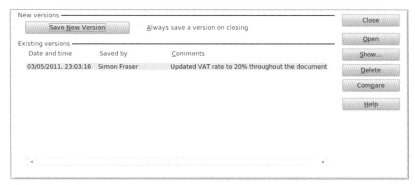

The version manager

6. Make some changes to your document, and then select **File** > **Versions...** again.

7. Select the version that you created from the list and select **Open**.

8. As you are opening a version of the current document you will be asked whether you want to open a read-only version or make a copy. Usually you will just want to open a read-only version so that you can refer back to the old version of the document.

9. The historical copy of the document will be opened in a new window and you will see that the old version does not include the changes made in step 5.

To create a new version of your document on every occasion that you close the document, check the **Always save a version on closing** checkbox in the **Versions of...** dialog.

Compare Documents and Find Differences Quickly and Easily

When you share documents you will find that others make changes. You can even find that different copies have been edited simultaneously. If the other parties have not tracked their changes it can be difficult to determine what has changed in your document – this is especially tricky when you need to work out the differences between a number of documents.

Fortunately, Writer allows you to make comparisons between documents. You can make comparisons between any two documents, but obviously the comparison works best when both documents are variations of a single original document. In addition, the comparisons can be composed; meaning that you can find the differences between any number of documents.

To quickly find the differences between three documents, do the following:

1. Open your copy of the document.

2. Select **Edit > Compare Document...**

3. Find the second copy of the document with the file chooser and select **Open**.

4. The **Accept or Reject Changes** dialog will appear. This will allow you to accept or reject changes in the same way as when using change tracking. If you wish to simply review the changes or, as in this case, compare a third document simply close the dialog.

5. Again, select **Edit > Compare Document...**

6. Find the third copy of the document with the file chooser and select **Open**.

7. The **Accept or Reject Changes** dialog will appear again. This will present all of the differences between the three documents. You will find that this is easy to understand as it will simply look as if someone has made changes with tracking on. You can now **Accept** or **Reject** the changes until your list is empty and you are left with a document that consolidates all of the changes made.

   If you close the **Accept or Reject Changes** dialog, you can reopen it at any time by selecting **Edit > Change > Accept or Reject...** as if the changes were the result of tracking.

You can easily compare your current document with its previous versions by selecting **File** > **Versions...** selecting an old version, and selecting **Compare**.

Add Variety to Your Document: Find Synonyms Quickly

When you are writing a document, it can be hard to avoid using the same words over and over again. Using more variation will make your document more compelling, and make it easier for the reader to understand. There are paper thesauruses, and numerous resources available on the Internet, but using one of these can really interrupt your writing flow. Writer comes with an integrated thesaurus that allows you to find a synonym with minimum interruption.

If you're using Ubuntu you may have trouble getting the thesaurus to work. To fix this see **Getting the GB Thesaurus Working on Ubuntu** on page 81.

To use Writer's in built thesaurus and quickly replace a word in your document, do the following:

1. Move your cursor to a word for which you would like to find a synonym.

2. Select **Tools** > **Language** > **Thesaurus...**

   Alternatively, pressing **Ctrl+F7** will bring up the **Thesaurus** dialog immediately. Pressing **F7** on its own will initiate a spell check on your document and pop-up the **Spelling** dialog if an error is found.

3. The **Thesaurus** dialog pops up and you will see a list of proposed words that could form a replacement for your word.

   Where a word can be used in a number of different ways you will see a list of numbered categories that describe those uses and the part of speech that is used in that context.

The thesaurus

4. Scroll through the list and find a suitable replacement for your word. Select the replacement from the list and select **Replace**.

5. The synonym will replace your word in the document and you will be able to continue editing immediately.

If you find a word that is almost what you want, but not exactly, then try double-clicking on that word in the list. This will ask the thesaurus to find synonyms for this word instead of your original word.

Save Time: Let Writer do the Typing

When writing, one of the hardest tasks can be just getting everything typed. It can be especially frustrating if you need to keep entering the same piece of text. The problem can be further compounded if you need to reapply the same formatting to that piece of text every time you type it.

AutoText is a tool provided by Writer that allows you to save time when you need to enter the same piece of text repeatedly. You can define an AutoText entry that will store a piece of text that will be retrieved whenever you use a defined shortcut.

AutoText is not just restricted to raw text; it can be used to store the formatting of the text. Graphics or tables can also be incorporated into an AutoText entry. To create and use an AutoText entry, do the following:

1. Select the section of the document that you wish to make an AutoText entry.

    Graphics can only be used within AutoText if they are preceded, and followed, by text.

2. Select **Edit > AutoText...**

3. The following screenshot shows the AutoText dialog. Type a name for your entry in the Name field. The name simply allows you to manage and identify your AutoText entries.

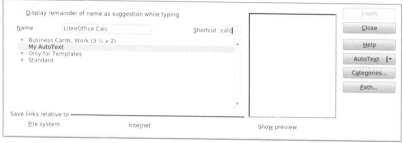

The AutoText dialog

4. Enter a shortcut for your entry in the **Shortcut** field. This will be the shortcut you use to retrieve the entry, so it should be short, but memorable.

5. Select the **AutoText** button and then select **New** from the drop-down menu.

6. Select the **Close** button. You will be returned to your document and you can continue working.

7. When you want to reuse the text stored as an AutoText entry, simply type the shortcut that you defined and then press **F3**. The shortcut will be replaced with the piece of the document that you selected in the step 1.

    If you can't remember the shortcut for an AutoText entry, select **Edit > AutoText** and then find your entry and select **Insert**.

Insert Captions Automatically

In addition to AutoText, there are other ways to get Writer to do the typing for you. If you are creating a large document with lots of pictures and you know that you are going to want to add captions to all of those pictures you can get Writer to add the captions automatically:

1. Select **Tool > Options**.

2. Expand the **LibreOffice Writer** subtree and select **AutoCaption**.

3. If you wish to automatically caption your pictures check the **LibreOffice Writer Picture** checkbox.

4. On the right-hand-side of the dialog choose the caption formatting that you would like to use throughout your document.

5. Select **OK**. Now, whenever you insert a picture into your document, a caption will be inserted; you will still need to insert any specific details, but most of the hard work is done.

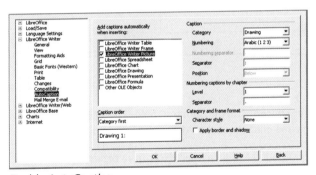

Enable AutoCaption

6. Expert Spreadsheet Know-how Using Calc

Navigate Through Your Spreadsheets with Ease

Whilst using the mouse allows you to move around your spreadsheet, you soon find that you can use the arrow, Tab and Enter keys to navigate more quickly. However, there is an abundance of additional keyboard shortcuts that can make navigating large spreadsheets a breeze.

General Shortcuts

The following table describes the most useful of the general shortcuts:

Key combination	Effect
Ctrl + 7 Home	Selects the first cell in the spreadsheet. This will always be the **A1** cell.
Ctrl + End	Selects the last cell on the spreadsheet that actually contains data. A spreadsheet can keep being extended as you need the space so there is no practical limit to the size of your spreadsheet.
7 Home	Selects the first cell in the current row. This will always be a cell in the **A** column.
End	Selects the last cell in the current row that contains data.
Ctrl + 9 Pg Up	Displays the next worksheet on the left. Does nothing if already in the first worksheet.
Ctrl + 3 Pg Dn	Displays the next worksheet on the right. Does nothing if already in the last worksheet.
Ctrl + ⇧ Shift + 9 Pg Up	Selects the next worksheet on the left in addition to any worksheets selected currently. Does nothing if already in the first worksheet.
Ctrl + ⇧ Shift + 3 Pg Dn	Selects the next worksheet on the right in addition to any currently selected worksheets. Does nothing if already in the last worksheet.

Key combination	Effect
[Alt] + [9 Pg Up]	Moves the viewable area of the spreadsheet one screen to the right.
[Alt] + [3 Pg Dn]	Moves the viewable area of the spreadsheet one screen to the left.

Using Data Ranges to Navigate Quickly

Data ranges are sequences of cells that contain data. For example, in row 1 of the spreadsheet shown in the following screenshot, there are two data ranges:

- **A1** to **C1**
- **E1** to **F1**

There are also two data ranges in column A. These are:

- **A1** to **A2**
- **A4** to **A6**

	A	B	C	D	E	F
1	1	2	3		4	5
2	2					
3						
4	3					
5	4					
6	5					
7						

Data ranges

The following keyboard shortcuts can be used to navigate using data ranges. These are very useful and very addictive and are well worth the time it takes to get to know how they work:

Key combination	Effect
[Ctrl] + [←]	If an empty cell or the leftmost cell in a row's data range is currently selected, will select the cell at the right end of the next data range to the left (or the first cell in the row if there are no data ranges to the left). If another cell within a data range is selected, will select the leftmost cell in the current data range.

Key combination	Effect
[Ctrl] + [→]	If an empty cell or the rightmost cell in a row's data range is currently selected, will select the cell at the left end of the next data range to the right (or the 'last' cell in the row if there are no data ranges to the right). If another cell within a data range is selected, will select the rightmost cell in the current data range.
[Ctrl] + [↑]	If an empty cell or the topmost cell in a column's data range is currently selected, will select the cell at the bottom of the next data range above (or the first cell in the column if there are no data ranges above). If another cell within a data range is selected, will select the topmost cell in the current data range.
[Ctrl] + [↓]	If an empty cell or the bottommost cell in a column's data range is currently selected, will select the cell at the top of the next data range below (or the last cell in the column if there are no data ranges below). If another cell within a data range is selected, will select the bottommost cell in the current data range.
[Ctrl] + [⇧ Shift] + [↑] or [↓] or [←] or [→]	Selects all the cells between the currently selected cell and the cell that would be selected by the appropriate action above.
[Ctrl] + [* 8]	Selects all the cells in the current data range.

The * key can be found on the numeric keypad available on most keyboards. Pressing the **Shift** key and the number **8** key will not produce the same effect.

Ensure Table Headings are Always Visible when Scrolling

When using a spreadsheet you are often producing a table, and frequently the spreadsheet contains a large amount of data such that you need to scroll about the spreadsheet in order to be able to see it all. When you create a table you usually assign row and column headings so that it is easy for everyone to see what the data means. Unfortunately, when you start scrolling, the carefully crafted headings can disappear from the screen.

Calc offers two solutions to this problem known as **Freeze** and **Split**. I would strongly recommend that you use the freeze technique as it prevents the same rows and columns being shown in your spreadsheet more than once. To freeze your spreadsheet, and stop headers moving off the screen, do the following:

1. Scroll the spreadsheet so that the start of your spreadsheet is visible. Usually this can be achieved by going to the spreadsheet's first cell.

2. Select the cell that belongs to the first row that does not contain headings and also the first column that does not contain headings. This would be **B2** in the following screenshot.

Select the cell for freezing

3. Select **Window** > **Freeze**.

4. You will see solid black lines appearing to the left of, and above, the cell that you selected. Now scroll the spreadsheet and observe that your row and column headings always remain visible.

A frozen spreadsheet

Make Your Spreadsheet Easier to Understand with Comments

There is often a need to fit a lot of data in a small amount of space on a spreadsheet. When creating things like forms you will want to keep all of the data within a relatively small area so that it can be printed on to a single piece of paper. In order to save space you inevitably leave out explanations so that there is more room for the raw data. When you do this, however, you end up with a spreadsheet that can be hard to understand.

Fortunately, Calc has a way in which you can add explanations to your spreadsheet without making it any bigger. Calc refers to these explanations as comments. Of course, comments can be used in any spreadsheet and they allow you to add lengthy notes without disrupting the shape of you spreadsheet. To add comments to your spreadsheet, do the following:

1. Select the cell that you want to add a comment to.

2. Select **Insert > Comment**

3. Enter the required explanation in the yellow comment box.

4. When you've finished, click on the spreadsheet. This will dismiss the comment. You will see that the top-right of the cell now has a small red square; this indicates that the cell has a comment.

5. When you hover over a cell with a comment for a few seconds the comment will appear as shown below.

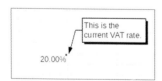

A comment on a cell

Once you have a comment in place there are a few actions that you may wish to perform on it. Some of these are described in the following table:

Action	Instruction
Show the comment on the screen all the time	You can toggle whether a comment is shown all the time by right-clicking on its owning cell and toggling the **Show Comment** checkbox in the context menu.
Move the comment	Move the mouse over the comment – the cursor will change into a four-arrowed cross – then click and drag the mouse to move the comment.
Resize the comment	Move the mouse to one of the comment's edges – the cursor will change into a dual-headed arrow – then click-and-drag the mouse to resize as required.
Edit the comment	While the comment is showing double-click it.
Delete the comment	Right-click on the comment's owning cell and select **Delete Comment** from the context menu.

Pressing **Ctrl+F1** quickly displays the comment that is attached to the current cell.

View Lots of Data in a Narrow Cell by Wrapping Text

When you have a large amount of data in a cell it can be difficult to see it all without making the cell's column very wide. An alternative is to increase the height of the cell. However, when you increase the height nothing appears to happen. In order to instruct Calc to make the best use of the height available do the following:

1. Select the cell(s) containing a large amount of data.

2. Select **Format > Cells**.

3. Select the **Alignment** tab.

4. Check the **Wrap text automatically** checkbox.

Wrapping text automatically

5. The **Hyphenation active** checkbox can be checked or unchecked. If hyphenation is active the wrapping can be more efficient, but some people do not like the aesthetics of the resulting text.

6. Select **OK**. The text in the cell will now be wrapped so that the text does not extend beyond the width of the cell; data too wide for the column will be shown on the next line.

When working with cells with a height that is greater than one line of text **Ctrl+Enter** can be used to start a new line. Note that, this key combination only works when editing the cell directly and not in the input bar at the top of the window.

If you have tall rows, it may be that not all the cells have enough data to fill the available height. When this happens, Calc defaults to showing the data at the top of the row. This is not always the best looking solution. Fortunately, you can control how the data is displayed by selecting an appropriate alignment from the drop-down list below **Vertical** on the **Alignment** tab shown in the screenshot above.

Ensure that All of a Cell's Data Can be Seen

Sometimes you want to be sure that you can see all of the data contained in a cell at a glance. You could wrap the text as described in the previous section, but you may not wish to make a whole row higher just to fit one cell's data in, and wrapping doesn't work particularly well with numbers. Fortunately, there is an alternative; Calc allows you to specify that a cell's data should always be compressed to fill a cell. This method works particularly well when you're only expecting the text to be slightly larger than the cell's width. For example, you may have a stock spreadsheet and you almost always have less than a hundred of each item, so you make the field wide enough to fit two digits. Very occasionally you get more than a hundred stock items, but you don't want to make the field wider as space is at a premium in your spreadsheet.

To ensure that a cell's entire contents are visible, do the following:

1. Select the cell containing all of the data.

2. Select **Format > Cells**.

3. Select the **Alignment** tab.

4. Check the **Shrink to fit** checkbox.

Shrink to fit

5. Select **OK** and you will see that your data will always be visible regardless of the width of the cell and the length of the text. Of course, if there is too much of a disparity the text will soon become so small that it is hard to see and a different approach will be required.

   The following screenshot shows the difference between a column without shrink to fit enabled – column **A** – and one where it is – column **B**.

	A	B
1	###	524
2	88	88
3	###	123
4	44	44
5		

Shrink to fit in action

To select all the cells in the spreadsheet click the top-left corner of the spreadsheet – to the right of A and above 1 in the previous screenshot. You can also achieve this by pressing **Ctrl**+**A**.

Paste Special: the Professional Way to Copy Data

You may think that copying and pasting is a relatively simple thing; you're just copying some data from one place to another. In Calc, however, things can get a bit more complicated and the unwary user can often be surprised by the results.

Each cell in Calc stores more than just a piece of text. There are formulas, references to other data, colours, comments, etc. all contained within a single cell. When you copy and paste, Calc can either copy some, or all, of this information.

When you use the standard copy and paste facility all of the information will be copied, but this can often lead to undesirable results.

For example, you may have used one spreadsheet to calculate an account's balance at the end of a month. You then copy this value into another spreadsheet where you wish to store all of the month-end balances over a year. Everything is fine until you reuse the first sheet to determine the next month's balance whereupon you realise that your spreadsheet's month-end balance has changed. You hadn't just copied the result of the calculation, but a formula that referenced the first sheet.

Fortunately, Calc provides a method for copy and paste that allows you to choose which pieces of data are copied; you copy in the usual way, but when you paste you use the **Paste Special** feature. The keyboard shortcut for Paste Special is **Ctrl+Shift+V**.

The following sections describe some of the advantages that using Paste Special can bring.

Copy the Results of a Formula so that its Value Does Not Change

As in the example above, you often want to copy the value of a calculation's result rather than the formula used to obtain it. To do this, do the following:

1. Select the cell containing the calculation whose value you wish to copy.

2. Select **Edit > Copy**.

3. Select the cell in which to place the result.

4. Select **Edit > Paste Special**.

5. Uncheck the **Paste all** checkbox so that you can control what information is pasted.

6. Check all of the checkboxes other than the **Formula** checkbox – as shown in the following screenshot. This will ensure that all data is copied other than the formula itself.

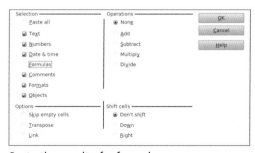

Paste the result of a formula

7. Select **OK** and you will find that the value of the calculation has been copied, but not the formula. You can check this by changing the values used to make the calculation and observing that your pasted value does not change.

Copy and Paste a Value without Losing the Existing Formatting

I'm sure you've encountered the situation where you have two areas of your spreadsheet with two different formats and you copy a value from one to the other and lose the formatting. You then need to spend time patching up the pasted cell so that it is formatted in the same way as its surrounding cells. Paste Special will allow you to paste the data so that you won't lose the original formatting. To use Paste Special in this way, do the following:

1. Select the cell containing the data to copy.

2. Select **Edit > Copy**.

3. Select the formatted cell in which to place the result.

4. Select **Edit > Paste Special**.

5. Uncheck the **Paste all** checkbox so that you can control what information is pasted.

6. Check all of the checkboxes other than the **Formats** checkbox. This instructs Calc to copy all data other than the formatting information which will ensure that the existing format is not overridden.

7. Select **OK** and you will find that your data has been copied, but your format preserved.

Convert a Long Row of Data into a Column in a Handful of Clicks

Converting a row of data into a column of data – or vice versa – is a more common operation than you might think. Changing data like this is commonly needed to convert column titles into row titles; for example, you may have a list of employee names as a row in one spreadsheet and you need them as a row in another. Obviously, you don't want to have to type them all in again so people look to use copy and paste. There are many times that I have seen someone try to convert a long row of data into a column by cutting and pasting one cell at a time from the right of the row to the bottom of a column, but this is almost as time-consuming as retyping the whole lot.

Fortunately, Paste Special will come to your rescue once again and save you a great deal of time. To convert between rows and columns of data, do the following:

1. Select the row of data to convert into a column.

2. Select **Edit > Cut**.

3. Select the start cell for the new column of data.

4. Select **Edit > Paste Special**.

5. Check the **Paste all** checkbox to ensure that all of the row's data will be retained.

6. Select the **Transpose** checkbox. This instructs Calc to convert rows to columns and vice versa.

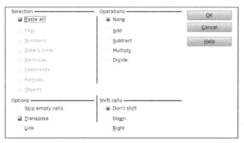

Transpose

7. Select **OK** and you will see that the row of data is now a column.

Add 1 Cell to Another without Using a Formula

Another feature of Paste Special is the ability to perform arithmetical operations on the data being pasted. You can copy one number and then paste the result of adding the copied number to the number present in the target cell. To achieve this, do the following:

1. Select a cell containing a number.

2. Select **Edit > Copy**.

3. Select another cell containing a number.

4. Select **Edit > Paste Special**.

5. Ensure that either the **Paste All** or **Number** checkboxes are checked so that the cell's value can be used.

6. Choose the **Add** option from the **Operations** section.

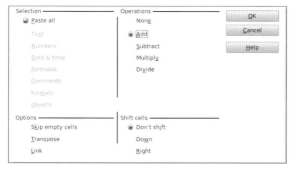

Perform an operation on paste

7. Select **OK** and you will see that the values of the cells have been added and placed in the target cell.

Take Control when Deleting

Each cell in the spreadsheet has more data than the value visible in the spreadsheet. When we press **Delete** in Calc some of a cell's data is deleted, but some of it is not. Usually Calc's default is what we want and it deletes pretty much everything except the formatting. However, there are some occasions where you want finer control over what's deleted.

> To delete a cell's formatting quickly and easily, select **Format** > **Default Formatting**.

Consider, for example, a situation where you have a spreadsheet that you're going to give to someone else, but you've attached a lot of comments to cells throughout the sheet that help you understand what's going on. These comments have just been written for you so you don't really want someone else reading them. You want to delete them, but you don't want to have to find every comment and remove it individually.

Calc offers a solution that offers great control over what's deleted. For example, you can delete a cell's contents and its formatting at the same time, or you can delete all the cells with text without touching those containing numbers.

To delete all the comments from a selection, do the following:

1. Select the cells from which you wish to delete the comments.

2. Press **Backspace**.

3. Uncheck everything except the **Comments** checkbox, as shown below.

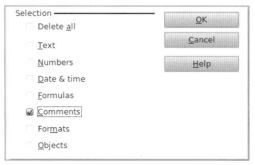

Advanced deleting

4. Select **OK** and you will see that all of the comments have been deleted, but the rest of the data remains intact.

If you press **Ctrl+Delete** with a cell selected, the cell's contents will be deleted and the cell opened for editing immediately.

Avoid Calculation Errors by Using Absolute References

When you insert a reference to another cell in a formula, Calc will use relative references by default. Generally, this is not a problem and may be exactly what you want, but sometimes you need to refer to a specific value from across your spreadsheet.

For example, you may wish to convert a list of prices to dollars. You would probably put the exchange rate between pounds and dollars in a cell so that it can be updated as the exchange rate changes. You would then use that cell to convert the first price in your price list. At this point you may have a spreadsheet like that shown in the following screenshot.

	A	B	C	D
1			Ex Rate	1.62
2				
3	Price 1		£23.00 =B3*D1	
4	Price 2		£8.50	
5	Price 3		£9.00	
6				

Creating a formula

What you would now expect is that you could copy the formula used for your first price, and use it to convert all of your prices. However, when you do this none of the conversions appear to work correctly, as you can see in the next screenshot.

	A	B	C	D
1			Ex Rate	1.62
2				
3	Price 1	£23.00	$37.26	
4	Price 2	£8.50	$0.00	
5	Price 3	£9.00 =B5*D3		
6				

Problems with relative references

The results of the calculations are not correct because the initial formula was created with relative references. When the data is pasted, Calc expects the cell containing the exchange rate to be relative to the current cell – appearing one column to the right of and two columns above the cell where each formula is defined.

To fix problems like this you must use absolute references within your formulas. To use an absolute formula do the following:

1. Select the cell in which to store the first calculation – here **C3**.

2. Select the first referenced cell by clicking on it in the normal way as you still want the price used to change for each calculation. In this instance, **=B3**.

3. Enter the required mathematical operation – here giving **=B3***.

4. Enter the location of the cell for which an absolute reference is required, but prefix both row and column reference with a **$** symbol. As the required cell in the example is **D1** you would enter **$D$1**, giving a final formula of **=B3*$D$1**.

5. Copy this formula into all of the required locations. The references will now be made correctly. The results of doing this in the example can be seen in the next screenshot.

	A	B	C	D
1			Ex Rate	1.62
2				
3	Price 1	£23.00	$37.26	
4	Price 2	£8.50	$13.77	
5	Price 3	£9.00	=B5*$D$1	
6				

Using absolute references

When working with a complex spreadsheet it can sometimes be easier to see the formulas within the cells rather than the results of the formulas. Pressing **Ctrl+`** will toggle between displaying formulas and results in all of a spreadsheet's cells.

Create Formulas More Easily by Giving Cells a Name

One of the difficulties with creating formulas in Calc is referencing other data. This becomes a particular issue when you are using a document with many sheets or sheets with large amounts of data. Every time you need to reference a cell you need to switch sheets or scroll the book to find the required data and select it to incorporate it into your folder. Of course, you could just type in the cell reference, but with names like **AA156** it is easy to get cells mixed up and you end up needing to double-check that you're referring to the correct cells.

Calc offers a solution. You are able to add more recognisable names to cells and commonly used ranges; so instead of referring to **D1** in your formula you can refer to **VatRate**. To assign a name to a cell or a range, and then use that name in a formula, do the following:

1. Select the cell or range of cells that you wish to name. In our example, this would be the cell **D1**.

2. Select **Insert > Names > Define**.

3. Enter a name in the **Name** field – here **VatRate**.

   Note that you can't include spaces when defining a name, so often underscores are used to make your names easier to read. For example, **rate_of_exchange** rather than **rateofexchange**.

4. Select **Add**. Your name appears in the list of defined names as shown below.

Defining a cell name

5. Enter your formula in the usual way, but instead of selecting the named cell, simply type it into the input bar. In our example, we would type **=B1*VatRate**

	A	B	C	D
1			VatRate:	20.00%
2				
3	Item:	Price (excl VAT)	VAT	Price (incl VAT)
4	Spade	£8.99	=B4*VatRate	£10.79
5	Fork	£7.99	£1.60	£9.59
6				

Using a defined name

When a name is assigned to a cell an absolute reference is used, so you can be sure that wherever it's referenced from, the correct value will be retrieved.

Remove Unwanted Clutter Using Look-up Tables

In many of the examples above we have used a single reference value in our calculations; such as VAT rate or exchange rate. However, you will often have a range of static data. For example, when calculating a payroll you may have staff with different pay grades where each grade earns a different hourly rate. If you include this data, as shown in the following screenshot, you end up repeating the hourly rate throughout your spreadsheet which not only clutters up your spreadsheet, but also makes it difficult to change that hourly rate easily. The problem is compounded when the grade affects a number of fields – for instance, an overtime bonus rate – and your spreadsheet can become full of redundant data.

	A	B	C	D	E	F
1		Grade	Hours	Rate	Overtime	Wage
2	John	3	35	£7.33	£0.40	£256.55
3	Steve	4	38	£8.42	£0.50	£321.46
4	Derek	2	40	£6.84	£0.30	£275.10
5	Will	3	35	£7.33	£0.40	£256.55
6	Janet	3	37.5	£7.33	£0.40	£275.88
7	Juliet	5	35	£9.23	£0.60	£323.05
8	Dave	2	37.5	£6.84	£0.30	£257.25
9	Mark	1	36	£6.25	£0.25	£225.25
10	Stephen	2	35	£6.84	£0.30	£239.40

A cluttered spreadsheet

To overcome this you need to create look-up tables and then use the **VLOOKUP** and **HLOOKUP** functions to retrieve the required data. To use a look-up table to reduce the unnecessary data in a spreadsheet, do the following:

1. Use a portion of your spreadsheet to create a table that contains the key and the values that depend upon it. In our example, the key is the grade and the values are the rate and the overtime rate. A look-up table for this example is shown below. The column headers do not form part of the table, but help you make sense of your data.

	A	B	C
1	Grade	Rate	Overtime
2	1	6.25	0.25
3	2	6.84	0.3
4	3	7.33	0.4
5	4	8.42	0.5
6	5	9.23	0.6
7			

A look-up table

2. Delete the columns that contain the look-up values in the initial spreadsheet. In the example, we delete columns **D** and **E** which contain the rates and the overtime rates.

3. Use the **VLOOKUP** or **HLOOKUP** function to retrieve the required data in a formula. These functions take three arguments: the key to search for, the location of the look-up table and the index of the value that you want to use.

   The key is the piece of information that you have, in this instance the grade.

   The location of the lookup table is the range of cells in which the table is defined. Look-up tables can be in the same worksheet, a different worksheet or in another spreadsheet altogether, but don't forget to use absolute references when defining the location of the look-up table or Calc won't be able to find your data.

   The index refers to the index of the column whose value you wish to return. Here you would want the value contained in the second column so the index required is 2.

   In this instance, we have defined our look-up table in a worksheet called **Rates** so to retrieve the value of the rate for John we would use **VLOOKUP(B2,Rates.$A$2:$C$6,2)**.

   The actual formula used to calculate the wages for each person in total, is shown in the screenshot below.

	A	B	C	D	E	F
1		Grade	Hours	Wage		
2	John	3	35	=(VLOOKUP(B2.Rates.		
3	Steve	4	38	$A$2:C6.2)*C2)+(C2-		
4	Derek	2	40	35)*VLOOKUP(B2.Rates.$A$2:C6.3)		
5	Will	3	35	£256.55		
6	Janet	3	37.5	£275.88		
7	Juliet	5	35	£323.05		
8	Dave	2	37.5	£257.25		
9	Mark	1	36	£225.25		
10	Stephen	2	35	£239.40		
11						

Using a look-up table

The indexes of the values in the look-up table effectively start from 2, as a value of 1 will retrieve the key itself. For example, in the table above if you have a grade of 2 and lookup the value with index 1, you will just get 2 back again as it is value of the grade returned.

Insert and Delete Cells with a Single Key Combination

Inserting and deleting cells are two of the more common actions that you will perform when using Calc. Fortunately, there are a couple of keyboard shortcuts that can make doing this easier. The only constraint is that to use the insert shortcut you need a keyboard with a number pad. This will be fine for most desktop users, but laptop and netbook users may be out of luck. The following table describes the appropriate key combinations:

Key combination	Effect
Ctrl + +	Inserts cells.
Alt + –	Delete cells (not just contents).

7. Create Professional Presentations with Impress

Navigate Through Your Slide Show Like an Expert

There is nothing worse than a slide show where someone asks a question and the presenter needs to keep coming out of the slide show in order to find one of the previous slides. Just as bad, is when the presenter tries to move quickly back through a few slides, but the fancy animations – that looked so good the first time through – slow things to a crawl. By learning a few keyboard shortcuts, you will be able to navigate rapidly around your slide show, and your presentation will be slick and easier to follow. The following table describes some of the most useful shortcuts for working with the slide show:

Key combination	Effect
F5	Starts the slide show.
Esc	Ends the slide show.
Space, N, →, ↓, Page Down or ←Enter	Plays the next animation. If there are no effects on the current slide then Impress will just transition plainly to the next slide.
←Backspace, P, ←, ↑ or Page Up	Replays the previous animation. If there are no effects on the current slide then Impress will just transition plainly to the previous slide.
Ctrl + Page Down	Transitions to the next slide with only the transition animation.
Ctrl + Page Up	Transitions to the previous slide with only the transition animation.
Alt + Page Down	Transitions to the next slide immediately without any animations.
Alt + Page Up	Transitions to the previous slide immediately without any animations.

Key combination	Effect
Home	Jumps to the first slide.
End	Jumps to the last slide.
B or < ,	Shows a blank, black screen until you press another key.
W or < ,	Shows a blank, white screen until you press another key.

Create a Suite of Slide Shows from a Single Presentation

When a topic is important enough to make a presentation about it, you will frequently find that you end up making more than one presentation on that topic. It is likely that the presentations will be made to audiences with different levels of knowledge and understanding, and you are probably going to have to fill different time slots. What you don't want to have to do is start from scratch each time, but it can be quite hard trying to copy and paste the slides between presentations while maintaining their order and the flow of your script. It gets even harder when you realise you need to update one of your slides, and you have to go through all the different versions to make the change.

Impress provides a tool that will allow you to take one presentation and use it to generate a number of other presentations. Usually, you will start with a version of your presentation that contains all of the necessary slides and use the custom slide show feature to use it as the basis for other shorter or slightly different versions. The big advantage of this feature is that you will only ever have one copy of each slide, regardless of how many versions it is in, so you will only have one place that you need to make any changes. To make a custom slide show from an existing presentation, do the following:

1. Select **Slide Show > Custom Slide Show**.

2. The **Custom Slide Shows** dialog will appear. Select **New** to create a new customisation of the current presentation.

3. Select one of the slides that you wish to use in your new slide show from the **Existing Slides** on the left and select **>>**. The slide will be copied to the **Selected Slides** list. This list shows the slides in the custom slide show. Continue to add slides until all the slides that you need are in the **Selected Slides** list as shown below.

Selecting slides for a custom slide show

4. You can reorder the slides in the **Selected Slides** by dragging and dropping them further up or down the list. This will change the order in which the slides will appear in the slide show.

5. When you have finished creating your custom slide show, select **OK**.

6. You will be returned to the **Custom Slide Shows** dialog. To view your new customisation, select it from the list, check the **Use Custom Slide Show** checkbox and select **Start**.

You can create additional custom slide shows in the same way, until you have a suite of presentations suitable for any audience and any occasion.

Pressing **Ctrl** allows you to select more than one slide at a time. Pressing **Shift** allows you to select a range of slides.

Automatically Keep Your Presentation's Calc Charts Up-to-Date

Often the charts you will want to use in your presentations have already been created elsewhere; typically in Calc. It's easy enough to copy and paste a chart from Calc into your presentation, but when you do this you are just getting a snapshot of the data. Often the data you are using is changing and so you end up having to keep copying and pasting the chart into your presentation. Unfortunately, there is no simple way provided by Impress that will allow you to insert a 'live' view of your Calc chart into your slide show. However, the following trick will allow you to achieve the same thing with little fuss. To insert a Calc chart into your presentation so that it updates automatically, do the following:

1. Create a new worksheet in your Calc spreadsheet.

2. Either create a new chart from your data or copy and paste an existing chart into this worksheet.

3. Move the chart as far as possible into the top left-hand corner of the worksheet and save the spreadsheet.

4. Open up your presentation in Impress and locate the correct place to insert the chart. Now select **Insert > Object > OLE Object**.

5. Select the **Create from file** radio button and then select **Search**.

6. Find your spreadsheet and select **Open**.

7. Check the **Link to file** checkbox so that the dialog looks like that in the next screenshot and select **OK**.

Embedding a Calc chart

8. Save and close your presentation, and then make some changes to the chart data in Calc.

9. Open your presentation. A dialog will appear asking you whether you wish to **Update all links?** you should select **Yes**. This will cause Impress to update your chart, and you will see that the changes made in Calc have been reflected on your slide.

If you are working on the presentation and the chart at the same time, the only way to force Impress to update the chart is by closing and reopening your presentation.

When saving your spreadsheet, the worksheet containing the chart must always be visible, otherwise when the links are updated in the presentation you will be likely to see chart data.

Be Prepared: Time Your Slide Show Properly

Usually, when you're making a presentation, you have a fixed period in which you must deliver it. In order to ensure your presentation is not too short or too long, you will need to rehearse it. The best way to prepare in this way is to know how much time you have available for each of the groups of slides that make up the sections of your presentation. Impress provides a useful tool that will allow you to see how long each portion of your presentation takes. To view timing information while you rehearse your presentation, do the following:

1. Select **Slide Show** > **Rehearse Timings**.

2. A clock will appear in the bottom left-hand corner of your screen that shows the time that has passed since the start of the presentation.

3. When moving to a new slide you can either click the slide to progress to the next slide without resetting the timer or, if you have reached the end of a section you wish to time, you can click the clock and the timer will be reset.

For an ultra-slick presentation you can use the timings you generate to transition slides automatically. Do this by selecting **Slide Transition** from the task manager on the right of the screen, switching your slides to **No Transition**, and setting **Advance Slide** to **Automatically after**, before rehearsing your timings.

Create New Presentations Quickly by Combining Your Existing Presentations

When you're working on a topic you are likely to make more than one presentation that covers it. Usually, you'll make one presentation that covers one area, and another that covers a different area. You may make several of these smaller presentations and then be required to make one big presentation that encompasses the topic as a whole. You could copy and paste the slides across, but that takes time and when one of your small presentations changes you'll be forced to update the big one manually. So, when you need to make a big presentation like this, simply do the following:

1. Create a new presentation that will form the base.

2. Select **Insert > File**.

3. The **Insert Dialog** will appear. Choose the first of your presentations and select **Open**.

4. At this point you can choose to insert some or all of the slides from the other presentation. You will usually just want to insert them all.

5. Make sure that the **Link** checkbox is checked. This will ensure that the slides in the big presentation are updated when the small presentation changes.

Combining presentations

6. Select **OK** and the slides will be added to your presentation.

7. Repeat the necessary steps until all of your small presentations have been incorporated and then edit your presentation until you have an overview that suits your needs.

You can really save time if you use this tip in combination with the **Custom Slide show** feature described on page 56. You can merge in all the slides you need and then pick and choose the best ones for your presentation to produce several overviews of different lengths.

Position Your Objects Exactly Where You Want them

It can be really frustrating when you insert an object – such as a picture – into your presentation, and you want to get it in exactly the same place that you inserted an object on the previous slide. For instance, you may have a series of graphs which are based on the same data, and you wish to show how the data changes over a period of months. The last thing you want is the graph jumping around as you progress through your slide show. In order to overcome this, Impress includes a feature that enables you to place guides on your slides that will help you position your objects. As these guides show up on every slide, you can be sure that your object will appear in the same place every time.

To have your objects appear in the same place on many slides, just complete the following steps:

1. If a ruler is not shown to the top and left of the slide, select **View > Ruler.**

2. Select **View > Guides > Display Guides** and then **View > Guides > Snap to Guides**.

3. Click on the ruler at the top of the slide and while continuing to press the mouse button, drag the mouse downwards. A horizontal line indicates where a guide will be placed. It is usual to place this guide at the top of where you want your objects to be positioned.

    Don't worry about getting it exactly right immediately, as you can move the guide by dragging it with your mouse at any time.

4. Click on the ruler at the left of the slide and while continuing to press the mouse button, drag the mouse rightwards. A vertical line indicates where a guide will be placed. It is usual to place this guide at the left of where you want your objects to be positioned, so the point where this guide crosses the horizontal guide will become the top-left corner of your object.

5. Drag your object so that the top-left corner is approximately at the point where the guides meet. When you let go of the mouse button, the object will be snapped to the guides as shown in the following screenshot.

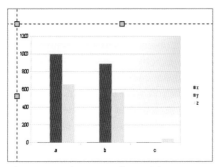

Placing an object on the guides

6. Move to your next slide and you will see that your guides remain in the same place. You can now drag your second object to the guides so that it is positioned in exactly the same place as the object on the previous slide.

   Using one set of guides in the top-left corner and another in the bottom-right will allow you to ensure that you have consistent size as well as position.

7. Once you have positioned all your images, you may not want to see the guides anymore. Simply select **View > Guides > Show Guides** and they will not appear on your slide. However, if you have another object to insert later on, you can just select **View > Guides > Show Guides** again and your guides will reappear.

To get exact control over the positioning and size of a single object, select the object and press **F4** and enter specific values into the **Position and Size** dialog.

Make Sense of the Data by Assigning Actions to Objects

When you have a long presentation with lots of objects inserted, it can be hard to keep track of where all the data has come from. You can use actions to link your objects to their source documents so that you can keep on top of all your data without needing to keep a load of documents open all the time. To enable you to open an object's source just by clicking on it, do the following:

1. Select the object.

2. Select **Slide Show > Interaction**.

3. Select **Go to document** from the **Action at mouse click** drop-down list.

You can assign other actions to objects, enabling you to play a sound when you click the item, go to another slide or run another application.

Assigning an action to an object

4. Select **Browse** and find the required document.

5. Select **OK** and then when you return to the presentation you just need to click on the object and your source document will open.

Make Risk-free, Last Minute Changes to Your Slide Show

Everyone's been there. You're making a presentation in five minutes and somebody's just told you that some of the data you're presenting can't be used, but it's right there in the middle of your presentation. Obviously you could start deleting slides, but that's not what you want to be doing with a few minutes to go – you may delete the wrong one and end up trying to restore from a backup.

To omit slides from your slide show while retaining them in your document, do the following:

1. Select **View > Slide Sorter**.

2. Right-click on any slides you wish to omit from the slide show and select **Hide Slide** from the pop-up menu.

3. Although the slides will still appear in the normal presentation view, when you start your slide show the hidden slides will be skipped.

4. If you no longer want a slide to be hidden, simply right-click on it and select **Show Slide** from the context menu.

You can also use the **Slide Sorter** to reorganise the order of your slides. Do this by dragging a slide into its new position.

8. Become a Data Management Expert with Base

Create a Database with Easy-to-Follow Steps

Base provides an efficient and professional solution for managing large data sets. Instead of struggling with one or many large spreadsheets from which it is hard to derive meaning, you can use a database that is designed to assist you in understanding your data.

Some people are put off Base because they believe it will be hard to use, but creating a database couldn't be simpler, just follow the straightforward steps below:

1. When you start Base, you will be presented with the **Database Wizard**, shown in the following screenshot. Ensure the **Create a new database** radio button is selected and select **Finish**.

Creating a database

2. You will be asked to provide a location to store your new database. Select a suitable filename and select **Save**.

That's it! You now have a database in which to store your data. The next thing to do is to create some tables.

Structure Your Database by Adding Tables

Databases use tables to provide structure to the data stored. For example, a table may be used to store details of all the people in the database. Each table has a number of columns and a number of rows. The columns store the attributes of the data and here this would be things like name, date of birth or hair colour. The rows form the actual data; so a single row may consist of John Smith, 1st February 1964 and brown. Each row typically has an id (also known as a primary key) that allows you to refer to that data in another table. For example, you may have a **person** table in which you store the id of the address from the **address** table at which they live.

> The terms **column** and **field** both refer to the same thing. They can be used interchangeably and frequently are. The choice of which term to use is mostly personal preference.

You will need to create some tables before you can store your data within the database. To do this, complete the following simple steps:

1. Select **Tables** from the launcher on the left of the window (as shown in the following screenshot).

The Base launcher

2. Select **Create Table in Design View** to bring up the **Table Designer**.

3. Enter the name of the first field and press **Tab**. Now, select an appropriate data type for the field.

    A data type describes what sort of data will be stored in the field. If you're not sure exactly what to use **Number**, **Text[VARCHAR]** and **Date/Time** should cover most of your needs and are fairly self-explanatory.

    Press **Tab** again to enter a description for the field. This is optional, but allows you to enter more details about what is stored in the field.

4. Repeat the above process for the other fields of the table. The following screenshot shows the result of doing this for the table used to store people described in the example above.

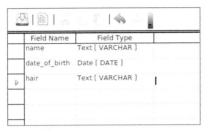

The Table Designer

5. Once all your storage fields have been created it is best to create an id field that can be used as a primary key. To do this, add a new field – typically called **id** or **<tablename>_id** – set the data type to **Integer** and then set the field property **AutoValue** to **Yes**.

Adding a primary key

When this is done correctly you will see a small key icon on the left-hand side of the field name.

6. Select **File > Save** and enter a suitable table name.

Note that conventionally the name of a table is singular rather than plural; for example, use book rather than books. In the example, a good name would be person.

If you did not create a primary key field above, Base will now ask you whether you wish to create one.

7. Close the **Table Designer** and add additional tables using the same process.

8. Your new tables will be shown in the bottom pane of the window. If you double-click on one of these, the **Table Data View** will be shown.

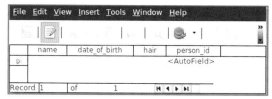

The Table Data View

9. You can now enter your data into the tables you have created in the same way as you would in a spreadsheet.

> When creating database tables and fields, the convention is to use underscores in the place of spaces – which are not allowed. So a field used to store first names may be called **first_name**.

Use Forms to Quickly Insert Data into Several Tables at Once

You may find that entering data in the **Table Data View** is not particularly efficient; this view has not really been designed for data entry and it shows. This becomes particularly apparent when you want to enter data about a single entity in more than one table. For example, you may want to enter data about a person in the **person** table, but also enter data in the **address** table.

Additionally, you may find that trying to explain how to use the **Table Data View** to someone who is less technically-capable can be quite difficult and they may also struggle with understanding the interface.

Fortunately, Base provides a way to create a more usable and professional interface to your data, giving you the capability to create **Forms**. Forms allow you to enter data into more than one table at once, and also enable you to present the form in a more user-friendly and professional way.

To create a form that allows you to enter data into two tables at once, simply do the following:

1. Ensure you have a field that links the two tables. For example, if you are linking a person and an address, the person table should have an **address_id** field that can be linked to the primary key of the **address** table.

2. Select **Tools > Relationships**.

3. The **Add Tables** dialog will be shown. Select each table that you wish to insert data into and select **Add**. When you have finished, select **Close**.

4. Select **Insert > New Relation**.

5. Ensure that the two tables are selected and then for each table choose the field that links them. For example, the screenshot below shows the linking of the **person** and **address** tables through the **address_id** field.

Defining a relation

6. Select **OK** and you will see the relationship displayed visually.

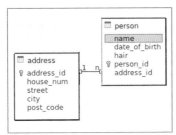

Visualising the relation

7. Save the relation and close the **Relation Design** dialog.

8. Select **Forms** from the launcher and select **Use Wizard to Create Form...**

9. Select the table for which the linking field is the primary key from the **Tables or queries** drop-down list. In our example, this would be the **address** table. Then select **>>** to copy all of the fields for use on the form, and select **Next**.

10. Check the **Add Subform** checkbox and then ensure the **Subform based on existing relation** radio button is selected and your relation is highlighted below. Select **Next** to continue.

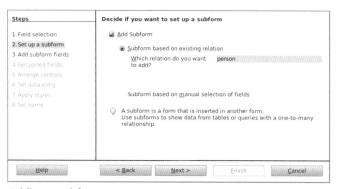

Adding a subform

11. Select the fields to include on the form from the second table and copy them using the **>** button. You would usually want all the fields except the linking field, which has already been included. Select **Next** to continue.

12. Choose how the form will be laid out. You can preview the effect of your choices by looking at the **Form Design** window. I prefer the **Columnar – labels on top view** as it gives a fairly simple layout that is easy to understand. When you are happy, select **Next** to continue.

13. You could now alter the data entry mode, but usually you will just want to skip this step by selecting **Next**.

14. At this point you can choose the theme for your form and this is a matter of personal preference. Again, the **Form Design** window will show you a preview. Select **Next** to continue.

The Essential Guide to LibreOffice

15. Add a name to the form and select **Finish**. Your form will now be shown and look something like the screenshot below.

The final form

16. You will now be able to use the form to view the existing data in your tables, make changes and insert new data.

The record toolbar at the bottom of the screen will allow you to scroll through the existing data and also to create new records.

Forms are also great ways to view your existing data as they allow you to display all the relevant data in a single window.

Create Professional Reports from Your Data

Forms and queries can be used to find data in your tables or to perform calculations. However, the results of forms and queries can only be viewed by users of Base, and can be impenetrable to the casual observer. Base enables you to create reports that give a view on your data that can be understood by anyone. Reports also allow for quick grouping of data. For example, if you have a table of expenses where each expense is allocated to a person, you can quickly produce a report that clearly shows the expenses grouped by the person they are allocated to.

To create a report that groups data, do the following:

1. Select **Reports** from the launcher on the left and then select **Use Wizard to Create Report...**

2. Select the table or query that you want to use for generating your report from the drop-down list below **Tables or Queries**.

3. Select the fields you wish to include in the report and select **>** to copy the appropriate fields. Normally, you will want to copy all of the fields except id fields – which will have limited value outside of the database. Select **Next** to continue.

4. You now have a chance to give your fields more sensible names for display. For example, you could label **date_of_birth** as **Date of Birth**. Enter a label for each field as you prefer and then select **Next**.

5. Select the field that you wish to group your report by and select **>**. In our example, you would want to group by the **name** field. Select **Next** to continue.

6. Your report will be automatically ordered by the field you have grouped by. If you want to add any additional ordering of the data you can specify it before selecting **Next** to continue.

7. Select a layout for your report. The results of choosing a particular layout can be previewed in the **Report Builder** window. Select **Next** to continue.

8. Enter a title for the report and select **Finish**.

9. The report will be opened in Writer and you will see your grouped data shown in a way that is clear and intuitive. Once you have your report in Writer, you can save it, print it or convert it to a PDF as you would any other Writer document.

At step 8 you can choose to format the report by selecting the **Modify report layout** radio button. This will enable you to add headers, footers and alter the layout of your report. While all of this could be done equally well in Writer, doing it here will ensure that when you generate the report again in the future, the formatting work will already be done.

PART 3

Get Rid of Frustrations: Tips for Getting the Best from LibreOffice

In Part 2, I showed you how to use LibreOffice to produce top-quality documents quickly. In Part 3, we'll cover some more-advanced topics, including how you can overcome some of the little niggles that prevent you getting things working *exactly* as you want them.

LibreOffice's Extension Manager is the first place to check when you run into trouble. If you're missing something, then the chances are that someone else was missing it too, and that somebody provided an extension to fill the gap.

Ordinarily, LibreOffice is fast enough, but if you have an old machine or are using particularly large documents – especially ones that include images – you may find that the application starts to slow down. This slowdown is easily prevented by taking advantage of some performance-boosting tips.

Part 3 also tackles some common issues in each of the LibreOffice tools. Some of these are the result of incompatibilities or oversights, and some just require a bit of know-how. In either case, the solutions covered in the following chapters will allow you to make your documents perfect.

And finally, being able to leverage the power of macros can save you a great deal of time and energy. You can record or program a series of actions and let the computer do all the hard work whenever you need to repeat them. Part 3 will show you how.

9. Don't Reinvent the Wheel: Extend the Suite

While using LibreOffice you may find yourself wishing for a piece of functionality that is not provided in the default installation. However, if you desperately need a new feature then it is likely that someone else will also have needed it. When many people need a feature like this, someone outside of the LibreOffice development team will often use their expertise to create extra functionality that provides the feature. In the spirit of the open-source community, these additional features are usually made freely available for you to download and install.

Get New Features with the LibreOffice Extension Manager

The LibreOffice Extension Manager, shown in the following screenshot, allows you to install additional features. To open the Extension Manager, select **Tools > Extension Manager...** from any LibreOffice tool.

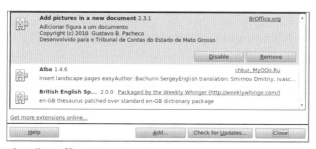

The LibreOffice Extension Manager

If you have previously used OpenOffice, you will probably be able to install any extensions that you used with it. You will find, however, that LibreOffice actually includes many of the most popular extensions by default. For example, the following popular extensions are included, and you will not need to install them manually:

- French, German and Spanish dictionaries (and more).

- PDF Import – allows you to import and edit PDF documents.

- Presentation Minimizer – reduces the file size of presentations.

- Presenter Console – discussed on page 97.

- Report Builder – generates professional database reports.

- Wiki Publisher – converts your documents into a format suitable for adding to a wiki (such as Wikipedia).

A growing, official list of additional extensions for LibreOffice can be found by clicking on the **Get more extensions online…** link in the Extension Manager. However, many more unofficial extensions can be found across the Web.

> Be careful when installing extensions from non-official sources as they will not have been checked by the LibreOffice team and may pose a security risk.

When you download an extension, you will simply need to double-click it in order to instruct LibreOffice to install it. For an example of installing a LibreOffice extension, see page 81.

Increase Your Productivity by Creating Many More Documents from Templates

Templates allow you to save a lot of time when creating your documents as they do a lot of the hard work for you. LibreOffice only provides a few templates when you first install it. Fortunately, there are many templates available to you on the Internet. The official LibreOffice template repository can be found at http://wiki.documentfoundation.org/Downloads/Templates. However, you are also able to take advantage of all the templates created for OpenOffice. You can find a repository of such templates at http://templates.services.openoffice.org/en.

When you have found a suitable template in one of these repositories, you will need to install it. To download and install a template from one of these repositories, do the following:

1. Use your browser to save the template from the repository.

2. In an applicable LibreOffice application, select **File > Templates > Organize**. This will bring up the **Template Management** dialog shown below.

The Template Manager

3. Right-click on **My Templates** from the list on the left, and then select **Import Template** from the context menu.

4. Find the downloaded template file and then select **Open**.

5. The new template will be added to the **My Templates** folder. Select **Close** to return to the application.

Once you have installed a template, you will need to create a document based on that template. This can be done in the usual way, as follows:

1. Select **File > New > Templates and Documents** to pop-up the **Templates and Documents** dialog shown below.

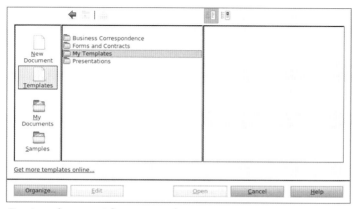

Create a document from a template

2. Select **Templates** from the list on the left.

3. Double-click the **My Templates** folder in the list on the right.

4. Select the template you wish to use from the list on the right and select **Open**. A new document will be created that is based on the template.

10. 3 Quick Tips to a Faster LibreOffice

Manage Your Memory to Make LibreOffice More Responsive

There are a number of variables that you can adjust that will alter the way in which LibreOffice uses your computer's memory. If you are using an older system, you may find that the following tips don't work quite so well and you may need to experiment with the values you enter until you get the best performance for your own system.

To get the best performance from LibreOffice, alter the memory management configuration as follows:

1. In any of the LibreOffice tools, select **Tools > Options**.

2. Expand the LibreOffice subtree, and select **Memory**.

3. For the variable **Graphics cache > Use for LibreOffice** enter **256**.

    As the title for this section of variables is **Graphics cache**, you may think that increasing the values will only help if you have graphics in your documents. In practice, however, the section appears to have been misnamed as the experience of many users has shown that significant performance is gained even in documents with no graphics.

4. For the variable **Graphics cache > Memory per object** enter **20**.

5. For the variable **Cache for inserted objects** enter **50**.

6. The dialog should now look like the screenshot below. Select **OK** and then close any LibreOffice tools that you have open. When you next open a LibreOffice tool you should have a much slicker experience.

Managing LibreOffice's memory

> If you're using an older system or are working with very large documents you can eke out a little more performance by reducing the values of the variable **Undo > Number of steps**. However, you need to be careful about reducing this too far as this is the number of actions that LibreOffice will be able to undo from the latest edit. For example, if you reduced the value to one, you would be unable to undo anything other than the last action you did.

Get the Best Performance by Installing the Latest JRE

Although LibreOffice doesn't absolutely require a Java Runtime Environment (JRE), having one installed is required for advanced features, and is certainly needed if you're using Base. If you're going to use a JRE you will want to ensure you are using the latest and fastest version as its performance will impact that of LibreOffice. The way to install the latest JRE depends upon your operating system.

Installing the Latest JRE on Windows

1. Open a web browser and go to: www.oracle.com/technetwork/java/javase/downloads.

2. Select **Download JRE**.

3. Select the radio box that says **Accept License Agreement**.

4. Select either the Windows x86 (for 32-bit versions of Windows) or Windows x64 (for 64-bit version of Windows) downloads.

5. Select either **Open** or **Run** from the pop-up dialog (depending upon your browser).

6. When the download has completed another dialog will appear, select **Install** to continue.

7. After a short while you will be greeted with a message telling you that you have successfully installed Java. Select **Close**.

Installing the Latest JRE on Ubuntu

1. Open a terminal.

2. If you're using Ubuntu 11.04 or later, type **sudo add-apt-repository "deb** http://archive.canonical.com/ **lucid partner"; sudo apt-get update** and press **Enter**.

3. Type **sudo apt-get install sun-java6-jre** and press **Enter**. You may need to enter your password at this point.

Update the JRE in LibreOffice

1. In any of the LibreOffice tools, select **Tools > Options**.

2. Expand the **LibreOffice** subtree, and select **Java**.

3. Ensure that the Use a Java runtime environment checkbox is checked.

4. LibreOffice will probably detect the newly installed JRE and show it in the list. If not, select **Add** and then browse to the location of the installed JRE.

   In Windows, this is usually **C:\Program Files\Java\<Java Version>**.

   In Linux, this is usually **/usr/lib/jvm/<Java Version>/jre**.

5. Select the radio button next to the JRE you have just added.

Choosing a JRE

6. Select **OK** and restart any open LibreOffice tools. You may not notice the performance advantages generally, but when it comes to using any of the features that are Java dependant such as Base, you will see a substantial improvement.

Ensure LibreOffice Launches Quickly by Doing the Hard Work During System Start-up

When you start up LibreOffice for the first time after switching on your computer you may notice that it can take quite a while to get going. The same is true if you close all of your LibreOffice documents and then reopen it. You can speed this up greatly by getting LibreOffice to start a daemon process when the computer starts-up. This allows LibreOffice to do a lot of the work it needs to do in the background during the start-up process. It also means that when you close all of your LibreOffice documents, the daemon process will remain running and make starting up again much quicker.

Complete the following steps to instruct LibreOffice to start the daemon process while the computer initialises:

1. In any of the LibreOffice tools, select **Tool > Options**.

2. Expand the **LibreOffice** subtree and select **Memory**.

3. Check the Load **LibreOffice during system start-up checkbox**.

4. Select **OK**.

11. Solve Common Issues with Writer

Use Windows Fonts on Ubuntu

When you start using LibreOffice on Ubuntu, you may be left wondering where Arial and Times New Roman have gone. Unfortunately, the standard Microsoft fonts are not available in a default Ubuntu installation due to licensing issues. However, getting access to these fonts is something that can be achieved quickly and easily. To install the Microsoft core fonts and get access to them within LibreOffice, simply do the following.

1. Select **Ubuntu Software Centre** from the launcher.

2. If you're using Ubuntu 11.04 or later, enter **ms fonts** into the search box and press **Enter**. Otherwise, search for **mscore**.

3. Select the entry **Installer for Microsoft TrueType Core Fonts** and select **Install**.

4. Once the installation is complete restart LibreOffice and you will find that the standard fonts are available.

The newly-installed fonts are: Andale Mono, Arial Black, Arial, Comic Sans MS, Courier New, Georgia, Impact, Times New Roman, Trebuchet, Verdana and Webdings.

Getting the GB Thesaurus Working on Ubuntu

Unfortunately, the default installation of LibreOffice on Ubuntu fails to install the British thesaurus correctly. Furthermore, it doesn't link to the US thesaurus so you are left without a usable thesaurus. However, you can install a quick extension to LibreOffice – that is available from our website – which will give you access to a British thesaurus.

To install the thesaurus, do the following:

1. Open your web browser and go to www.run-linux.co.uk/Libreoffice and select GB Thesaurus Extension.

2. A pop-up window will appear that asks whether you wish to open or save the file. You should choose to **Open with LibreOffice**.

The exact text will depend on the browser used, but the following screenshot shows how this appears in Firefox.

Opening a file downloaded with Firefox

3. After a few seconds the extension will be downloaded and LibreOffice will be opened. You will be asked whether you wish to install the extension. Select **OK**, and the extension will be installed.

Confirming the installation

4. Select **Close**, restart LibreOffice, and you will now have access to a British thesaurus.

Deactivate Automatic Link Creation

When you type something that resembles a URL – such as www.libreoffice.org – you will find that Writer automatically makes the text a link to the indicated web page and formats the text like an HTML hyperlink. While this works well in documents that are read primarily on a screen, when you are creating documents that will mostly be printed it can look a bit odd and break the flow of your text.

To stop Writer creating links automatically, complete the following steps:

1. Select **Tools > AutoCorrect Options...**

2. Select the **Options** tab.

3. Uncheck both checkboxes that appear in the row containing **URL Recognition**. The dialog should now appear similar to that shown in the next screenshot.

Disabling URL recognition

4. Select **OK**. You will be returned to your document, and when you next enter a URL a link will not be created.

Even with automatic link creation disabled, you can insert a link manually by selecting **Insert** > **Hyperlink**.

Change the Default Text Font

If the first thing you do every time that you create a new Writer document is to change the font face or size of the Default or Text Body styles, then you need to change the default font. The built-in styles use this font as a base so you do not need to worry about changing styles, and your new default will apply to all future documents (until you change it again).

To change the default text font, just do the following:

1. Select **Tools** > **Options**.

2. Expand the LibreOffice Writer subtree and select **Basic Fonts (Western)**.

3. A dialog similar to that shown in the next screenshot will appear. In the **Default** row select the required font face from the **Font** drop-down list and the new default font size from the **Size** drop-down list.

Changing the default font

4. Select **OK**. You will be returned to your document to find that your text has adjusted to the new default. Furthermore, when you open a new document your default will remain.

 You can also adjust the default font on which headers are based as well as the default fonts for captions, list and indexes.

Customise the Way a Date is Displayed

When inserting a static date reference, you enter the date in any format you want. When inserting a dynamic date reference – such as 'today's' date – the date will typically be displayed with the default format for your locale.

To change the way in which today's date is displayed, do the following:

1. Select **Insert > Fields > Other**.

2. Select **Date** from the list under **Type**.

3. Select **Date** from the list under **Select**.

4. The next screenshot shows how the dialog should now look. Select your preferred format from the list under **Format**. If none of the predefined formats are suitable select **Additional formats** from towards the end of the list, and create your own format.

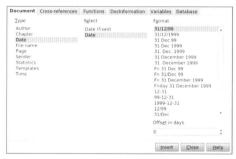

Customise the date format

5. Select **Insert** and then **Close**. Today's date will be inserted into your document with the correct format and will be updated correctly as the data changes.

To insert a dynamic date other than today, use the **Offset in days** variable. For example, for tomorrow use **1**, for yesterday use **-1** and for a week from today use **7**.

Increase Security by Protecting a Section from Changes

You may have a document that you want to share with others and while you would like them to make changes to some of the content, there are other parts that you would like to protect. Writer has the notion of **sections**. Sections are demarcated portions of your document for which you can define specific properties. One of the properties that you are able to control is whether the section is editable.

To prevent somebody else from changing a section of your document, complete the following steps:

1. Select **Insert > Section**.

   You will see a demarcated area placed into your document.

2. If you have already written the portion of the document that you wish to protect then cut and paste it into the demarcated area.

3. Select **Format > Sections…**

4. Check the **Protected** checkbox and the **With Password** checkbox.

    You can also use this feature more simply to prevent yourself accidently editing important passages. In this instance, you would probably just add the protection without a password.

Adding write protection

5. When you check the **With Password** checkbox, a password dialog will appear; enter and confirm a suitable password and select **OK**.

6. Select **OK** in the **Edit Sections** dialog.

7. When you return to the document and try to edit the text in the section you will see that you are prevented from doing so. Furthermore, if you try and turn the protection off, you will not be able to do so without entering the specified password.

Note that, whilst the protection described here will prevent honest mistakes and deter the nuisance, a committed fraudster would be able to circumvent these protections and so this security should not be relied upon to guarantee the security of your document and you should always proofread your documents to check that unwanted changes have not been made.

Add Page Numbers to Your Document

Those who have previously used MS Word are frequently stumped about how to insert page numbers into their document. Inserting page numbers in your LibreOffice document is not actually very difficult; it can just be hard to figure it out the first time.

To add page numbers at the bottom of your document's pages, just complete the following steps:

1. Select **Insert > Footer > Default**.

   If you wanted to insert the page numbers at the top of each page you would select **Insert > Header > Default** at this point.

2. Select the footer at the bottom of the document.

3. Select **Insert > Fields > Page Number**.

4. Use the normal formatting tools to place the page number in the desired location.

If you want to use a non-standard style for your page numbers – for example, roman numerals – replace step 3 with the following:

1. Select **Insert > Fields > Other**.

2. Select **Page** from the list under **Type**.

3. Choose a format for the page number from the list under **Format**. For roman numerals, there is a choice – shown below – select the one you prefer.

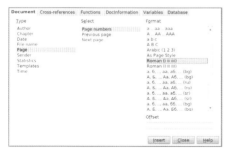

Using Roman numeral page numbers

4. Select **Insert** and the page number will be inserted into the footer, then select **Close**.

> Pressing **Ctrl+F2** will bring up the field management dialog enabling you to insert a wide-range of fields including any user-defined values.

Managing Automatic Word Completion

LibreOffice will try and automatically complete common words, for instance, if you type **Libr** into a document you will see that Writer will complete it to **LibreOffice**. Sometimes this is the correct behaviour, but every so often you will want another word. In either case, the feature can be quite annoying unless you are aware of how to take best advantage. When an automatic completion is suggested use the keyboard shortcuts in the following table to accept or reject the suggestion:

Key combination	Effect
Delete	Rejects the suggestion. Especially useful when entering a shorter form of an auto-completed word.
←Enter	Accepts the suggestion and moves the cursor to the end of the word.

By default, Writer will collect words that you use most often and add them to its word completion list. To remove words from this list, to stop Writer automatically adding words, or even to turn auto-complete off altogether, do the following:

1. Select **Tools > AutoCorrect Options…**

2. Select the **Word completion** tab.

Managing word completion

3. To remove a word from the word completion list, select it in the right-hand list and select **Delete Entry**.

4. To stop Writer collecting new words, uncheck the **Collect words** checkbox.

5. To stop Writer auto-competing as you type, uncheck the **Enable word completion** checkbox.

6. Select **OK** to return to your document.

12. Get Calc Working How You Want it

Understand Your Problem: Deciphering the Error Codes

Even a casual user of a spreadsheet program, such as Calc, quickly encounters one of the dreaded error codes. With messages like **#DIV/0!** and **Err:508** it can be easy to see why these codes leave people bewildered. The following table describes some of the more common error codes and explains how you may be able to fix them:

Error code	Explanation
###	The cell is not wide enough to display its contents. Make the column wider, shrink to fit or wrap the text.
Err:501	A character in the formula is invalid. I have found that this usually happens when people familiar with Excel use **;** instead of **,** as a separator in functions.
Err:502	An argument to a function is not valid. You will need to check what functions you are using and read their documentation to ensure that you are giving the correct arguments. For example, the square root function requires that all of its arguments must be positive numbers.
Err:503 **#NUM!**	The number is too big for the computer to hold in its memory. This can happen because the number is too large or has too many decimal places. However, I have found that the commonest cause of this error is that arithmetic is being performed on cells that are not numbers. Check that all of the numbers in your spreadsheet are considered numbers by Calc by selecting **Format > Cells** and checking that **Text** is not selected in the **Number** tab.
Err:504	An argument to a function is not suitable. In practice, this usually means that you have given text to a function that requires a number.
Err:508	Pair missing. This usually means that you've forgotten a bracket in your formula. For example, **=4*8)**.
Err:509	Operator missing. This usually means that you've forgotten a mathematical symbol. For example, you may have **=(48*50)100** when you meant **=(48*50)/100**.

Error code	Explanation
Err:510	Variable missing. This usually means that you have two mathematical symbols next to each other. For example you might have **=3*/4**.
Err:511	Parameter missing. This usually means that you have called a function with too few arguments. For example, **=SQRT()**.
Err:519 **#VALUE**	Result is not of the correct type. In practice, this usually means that you have passed a reference to a field declared as text to a function that requires a number.
Err:522	Circular reference. This means that you are either referencing the cell in its own formula or you have managed to create a loop. For example, having the formula **=A1** in the cell **B1** and having the formula **=B1** in the cell **A1**.
Err:524 **#REF**	Invalid references. One of the references you have made refers to a location that is no longer available. This often happens when you delete a worksheet that other worksheets depend upon.
Err:525 **#NAME?**	Invalid name. You have used some text like a name defined for a cell, but that name has not been defined. For example, **=SQRT(invalid_name)**.
Err:532 **#DIV/0!**	Division by zero. First check any divisions in your formula to ensure that you are not dividing by zero at any point. If this isn't the case, check that you have the correct arguments to any functions used as some of the supplied functions can cause this error if they divide by zero internally.

Get Your Headings Displayed on Every Page when Printing

When your spreadsheet crosses over more than one page you will probably find that, when you print, your row and column headers will only be shown on the first page that they appear. This can make data on later pages hard to understand.

To ensure that row and column headers are printed on every page, complete the following simple steps:

1. Select **Format > Print Ranges > Edit**.

2. The next screenshot shows the **Edit Print Ranges** dialog. Select – **user defined** – from the drop-down list under **Rows to repeat**.

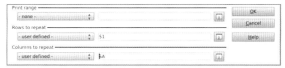

Managing print ranges

3. Return to your spreadsheet while leaving the dialog open and select a cell from your spreadsheet in the row containing the column headings.

4. Select – **user defined** – from the drop-down list under **Columns to repeat**.

5. Return to your spreadsheet while leaving the dialog open and select a cell from your spreadsheet in the column containing the row headings.

6. Select **OK** and you will find that when you next print your headers will be shown on every page.

> You can have more than one row or column repeated, but they must be adjacent and you must select them as a range.

Emphasise Your Data by Removing the Grid Lines

A lot of people use spreadsheets for more than just making complex calculations. Frequently, Calc is used for creating forms such as expense forms or timesheets. When printing a spreadsheet, the grid is not shown as it distracts from the core data. Nowadays, most forms are completed electronically, and a spreadsheet is just sent by email for completion. In this instance, the grid will again form a distraction as the structure is usually provided by the spreadsheet's format and structure.

When grid lines are not present it is clear which parts of the spreadsheet are relevant and the document looks more professional. Calc will allow you to change the colour of the grid lines to make them less off-putting, or even hide them altogether. To hide the grid lines in Calc, complete the following steps:

1. Select **Tools > Options**.

2. Expand the **LibreOffice Calc** subtree and select **View**.

3. Uncheck the Grid lines checkbox.

   If you just wish to change the colour of the grid lines, then keep the checkbox checked and select a new colour from the drop-down list immediately below.

Removing grid lines

4. Select **OK** and you will see that the grid lines disappear.

Finding Hidden Rows and Columns

If someone has hidden a row or column in a spreadsheet it can be hard to tell. Furthermore, it can be tricky to identify which row or column has been hidden, and then selecting that row or column so that you can show it again. When a row or column is hidden, the border between its neighbours becomes a little thicker – as shown in the following screenshot– but the easiest way to tell is that there is gap in the naming – here column **B** jumps straight to **D**.

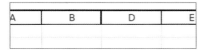

A hidden column

To show a hidden row or column, simply do the following:

1. Select a range of rows or columns that includes both the row/column before the hidden one and the row/column after it.

2. Select **Format > Row > Show** or **Format > Column > Show** as required. The hidden row/column will appear.

To quickly show all hidden rows and columns in a spreadsheet, complete the following steps:

1. Press **Ctrl+A** to select all of the cells in the sheet.

2. Select **Format > Row > Show** to show all the hidden rows.

3. Select **Format > Column > Show** to show all the hidden columns.

To hide a row or column, simply select a cell in the required row/column and then select **Format > Row > Hide or Format > Column > Hide as appropriate**.

Stop the Automatic Capitalisation of Text

When you're entering text into Calc and you don't want the first letter to be capitalised, you will probably get annoyed as you keep having to correct Calc's auto-capitalisation. To turn off the automatic capitalisation of the first word in a cell, simply do the following:

1. Select **Tools > AutoCorrect Options…**

2. Select the **Options** tab.

3. Uncheck the **Capitalize the first letter of every sentence** checkbox.

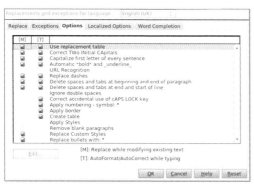

Disabling auto-capitalisation

4. Select **OK** and Calc will no longer correct you.

Add Long Titles to Your Spreadsheet

Spreadsheets are often used to create forms. When doing this – or even at other times – you regularly want to add a large title at the top of the spreadsheet. It can be quite hard to work out which cell to put the title in; the title can be longer than a single cell and you may want the title centred.

To add a long, centred title to your spreadsheet, complete the following steps:

1. Insert a row at the top of your spreadsheet to hold the title, by selecting row **1** and selecting **Insert > Rows**.

2. Select cells from the new row, such that the range covers the width of your spreadsheet.

3. Select **Format > Merge Cells > Merge and Center Cells** and select **Yes**. The selected cells will be merged into one and the new long cell will be centre-justified.

4. Enter your title into the long cell and you will find that it is placed correctly in the centre of your spreadsheet.

To break up a long cell, select it and then select **Format** > **Merge Cells** > **Split Cells**.

Make Your Form Secure

We have described above how Calc has become a useful tool for creating forms and distributing them electronically for completion. When you are distributing Calc forms you will usually want the form's recipient to only be able to enter their data in the cells provided. Without this protection, users are easily able to change your formulas, altering your calculations, and potentially committing fraud.

Calc provides a protection mechanism that will allow you to create a form that stops others making any changes other than inputting the data that you require from them.

To secure a Calc spreadsheet leaving only form input cells editable, complete the following simple steps:

1. While pressing and holding the **Ctrl** key, select all cells that you wish to allow someone to enter data.

2. Select **Format** > **Cells**.

3. Select the **Cell Protection** tab.

4. Uncheck the **Protected** cell.

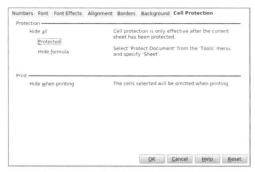

Removing protection from form cells

5. Select **OK**.

6. Select **Tools** > **Protect Document** > **Sheet**.

7. Enter and confirm a suitable password.

8. Uncheck the **Select locked cells** checkbox. This will prevent users being able to select the cells to which you don't want to give access. This means that others cannot see your cells' formulas as well as not being able to edit the locked cells.

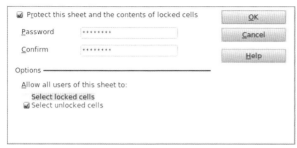

Disallowing the selection of locked cells

9. Select **OK**. You will now find that you can only select the form input cells. You will also be unable to select the remaining cells in the spreadsheet and so you will certainly be unable to edit them.

10. When you wish to make changes to your form, just select **Tools > Protect Document > Sheet** again and enter your password. Don't forget to re-protect it when you have finished!

Note that, whilst the protection described here will prevent honest mistakes and deter the nuisance, a committed fraudster would be able to circumvent such protection and so this security should not be relied upon to guarantee the security of your spreadsheet and you should always double-check suspicious data.

Change the Way the Enter Key Works

Usually pressing the **Enter** key in Calc moves the selected cell one cell down. While this can often be what you want, if you regularly have to enter rows of data you may find yourself wishing that the **Enter** key would move you to the right instead. Fortunately, it is pretty simple to make this change:

1. Select **Tool > Options**.

2. Expand the **LibreOffice Calc** subtree and select **General**.

3. Select **Right** from the drop-down list next to **Press Enter to move selection**. At this point, you could actually choose to move the selection left or up, but down and right are the usual choices.

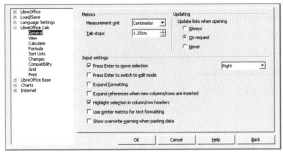

Change the Enter Function

13. Get Even More from Impress

Deliver a Note-free Presentation with the Presenter Console

Have you ever made a presentation and wished you had a tele-prompter like the professionals? Well, Impress doesn't quite give you that, but it can give you something pretty close. The Presenter Console allows you to use the screen of the computer on which you are running the presentation to view your notes while the projector still displays your slide show. Not only will you get to see your notes, but also the current slide, the next slide, the current time and the time passed since the beginning of the presentation, as shown in the following screenshot.

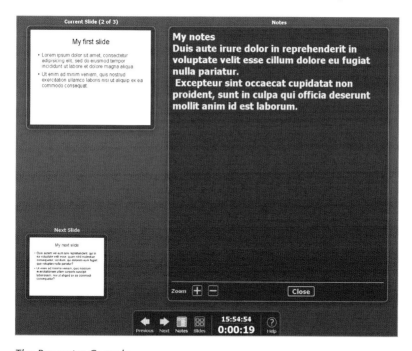

The Presenter Console

The Presenter Console will be started automatically on your primary screen if your computer has been set up to use two screens. You may find that this just works when you plug the projector in, but usually you will need to configure your machine.

Configuring a Second Screen in Windows

1. Connect your projector.

2. Right-click on the desktop and – depending upon your version of Windows – select **Display** or **Screen Resolution**.

3. Select **Extend these Displays** from the drop-down list besides **Multiple displays**.

Multiple displays in Windows

4. Select **OK** and start your presentation.

Configuring a Second Screen in Ubuntu

1. Connect your projector.

2. Select **Applications** from the launcher and search for **Monitors**.

3. Ensure the **Same image in all monitors** checkbox is not checked.

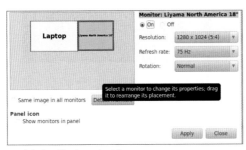

Multiple displays in Ubuntu

4. Select **Apply** and start your presentation.

Keyboard Shortcuts in the Presenter Console

The following keyboard shortcuts will give you greater control over the Presenter Console, by allowing you to toggle the display of various items:

Key combination	Effect
Ctrl + 1	Toggles the display of the Presenter Console.
Ctrl + @ 2	Toggles the display of the presentation notes.
Ctrl + # 3	Toggles the display of the slides overview.

Create an Interactive Video of Your Presentation that Can be Viewed on the Web

Making a presentation is great, but sometimes there are people who can't be there in person. You could email everybody who wanted to come with a copy of your presentation, but then you need to worry about what format to use and there's no guarantee that you'll be aware of everyone who might be interested. A better solution is to create an interactive video of your presentation. This video can then be put on a website and anyone who wants to will be able to view the presentation through their browser.

To convert your presentation into an interactive, Macromedia Flash video is simple, just complete the following steps:

1. Select **File > Export...**

2. Enter a filename and location for the video file.

3. Select **Macromedia Flash (SWF)** from the **Save as type** drop-down.

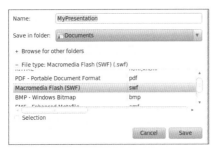

Create a Flash video

4. Select **Save**.

5. Start a browser and open the file you have just saved. Assuming that your browser has the Flash plugin, you will now be able to navigate your presentation in the browser.

   To make the presentation on the Web, simply upload the file you have created to a web host.

To install the Flash plugin in Windows, simply open the page http://get.adobe.com/flashplayer/ in your browser, select **Download Now** and when the dialog appears select **Open** or **Run**. Select **Yes** when Windows asks whether you'd like to confirm the installation. Next, check the checkbox which asks you to confirm that you've read the terms and conditions, close all of your browsers and select **Install**. When the installation is complete, select **Done**. You can now restart your browser and view your presentation.

Install Flash

To install the Flash plugin in an Ubuntu system close all your browsers, open a terminal and type **sudo apt-get install ubuntu-restricted-extras** and press **Enter**. When the install is done, you will be able to view your video in a browser.

14. Resolve Issues with Base

Avoid HSQLs Pitfalls: Connect to MySQL

HSQL is the default database system for LibreOffice Base. It is used because it is freely distributable, simple to install and easy to administer. While HSQL is fine for small examples, when you use it more extensively you will find that your data can become corrupted. If you're planning to use Base for something important you need to consider using one of the other databases supported by Base. Alternative back-ends include MySQL, PostgreSQL and MS Access.

MySQL is a free database that can be installed quickly and easily and has become one of the most widely used databases. Full instructions on installing MySQL can be found at: http://dev.mysql.com/doc/refman/5.5/en/installing.html.

When you have MySQL on your system or you have access to a MySQL database elsewhere (many Internet hosting services will provide you with a MySQL database in your hosting package), you will also need to install the MySQL JDBC connector, which will allow LibreOffice to communicate with the MySQL database.

Install the MySQL JDBC Driver on Windows

1. Open a browser and go to: www.mysql.com/downloads/connector/j/.

2. Select **Download** for the ZIP archive and open the file.

3. After the file has finished downloading, your default archive manager will be opened. Extract the contents of the ZIP file to somewhere memorable; I usually use **C:\Program Files\MySQL**.

Install the MySQL JDBC Driver on Ubuntu

To install the MySQL driver on Ubuntu, simply do the following:

1. Open a terminal.

2. Type: **sudo apt-get install libmysql-java**

Connect to a MySQL Database with Base

Once MySQL has been installed you need to instruct Base to use it instead of HSQL. You can do this by competing the following steps:

1. Select **Tools > Options**.

2. Expand the **LibreOffice** subtree and select **Java**.

3. Select **Class Path**.

4. Select **Add Archive** and browse to the file **mysql-connector-java.jar** (there may some additional version information in the filename) and select **Open**.

    In a Windows installation this file will be in the folder to which you extracted the ZIP file above.

    In an Ubuntu installation this file will be located in **/usr/share/java**.

5. Select **OK** and you will be asked to restart LibreOffice.

6. Once LibreOffice has closed, start-up Base again.

7. In the **Database Wizard** – shown in the following screenshot – select the **Connect to an existing database** radio button and select **MySQL** from the drop-down list below and select **Next**.

The Database Wizard

8. Ensure that the **Connect using JDBC** radio button is selected and select **Next**.

9. Enter a database name and server. If you haven't set up a specific database in MySQL, just enter **test** which is the name of the default database. For server you will usually want **localhost**.

10. Select **Next** and then enter your MySQL username. If you haven't set one up explicitly then use root which is the default username. Check the **Password required** checkbox unless you have configured the database not to need one.

11. Select **Next** and then select **Finish**.

12. The **Save As** dialog will appear and you will be prompted to store the details of your new database. Select an appropriate location and select **Save**.

13. The **Authentication Required** dialog will appear and you will need to enter the password for the user you selected earlier and then select **OK**.

14. You can now use Base as normal, but with the reassurance that your data is being stored in a professional database. As well as this security, using MySQL as your backend will allow you to use its plethora of tools that can allow you to interact and administer your database more easily.

Track Your Data with Timestamps

When you're storing your data in a database you will frequently want to record exactly when you inserted each piece of data. If you try to do this manually, you will find yourself having to do a lot of typing. In addition, you will need to constantly remember the exact date format used.

It is possible to instruct Base to populate a timestamp field for you automatically by using the following simple steps:

1. Create your table in the usual way, making sure that you include a field to store a timestamp. This field needs to have a type of **Date/Time [Timestamp]**.

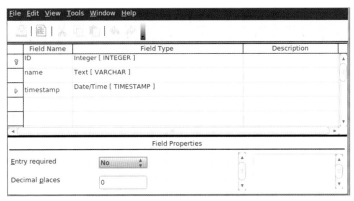

Adding a timestamp field

2. Switch back to the main window and select **Tools > SQL**.

3. Enter the following text and select **Execute**. The exact syntax depends upon which back-end you are using.

   For HSQL use: **ALTER TABLE "TableName" ALTER COLUMN "FieldName" SET DEFAULT CURRENT_TIMESTAMP**

   For MySQL use: **ALTER TABLE TableName CHANGE FieldName TIMESTAMP DEFAULT CURRENT_TIMESTAMP**

   You will need to replace **TableName** and **FieldName** with the name of your table and the timestamp field respectively.

4. Select **Close**.

5. Select the **Tables** view from the launcher and then double-click on your new table to insert some rows.

6. Enter your data as normal, but skip over the field used for the timestamp. When all the data has been entered for the row, the timestamp will be populated automatically with the current date and time. This can be seen in the next screenshot.

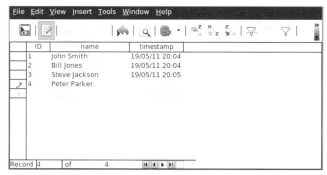

Entering data

Using Wildcards to Create Sophisticated Queries

For those who have not used a database or SQL before, it can be difficult to find data where a text field does not match a criterion completely. Finding data that only partially matches a criterion is a vital tool when querying a database. For example, you may have a name field that contains a person's full name and want to find all those people whose name contains **John**.

Furthermore, as the syntax in MS Access is slightly different, many Base users who have previously used that application will run into trouble when trying to create advanced queries that use wildcards.

To create a query using wildcards, do the following:

1. Select **Queries** from the launcher on the left of the screen.

2. Select **Create Query In Design View**.

3. Add the table that you wish to query by selecting it in the list and selecting **Add**, then select **Close**.

4. Select the field that you wish to search on from the **Field** drop-down list. For example, select the **Name** field from a **Person** table.

5. In the Criterion box type: **LIKE '%** followed by the fragment you wish to search for, followed by: **%'**. For example, when looking for John type **LIKE '%John%'**

The % wildcard can be replaced by the * used in MS Access, but the % symbol is what is used in the underlying database, and so understanding this syntax will help you if you need to view the SQL query.

Your query should look similar to the one shown below.

Creating the query

6. Save the query and press **F5**. This will run the query and you will see that it matches all the rows in which the fragment is contained within the field.

To find all rows where the fragment appears at the start omit the first **%** wildcard and to find all the rows where the fragment appears at the end omit the second **%** wildcard.

15. Save Time by Creating Macros in LibreOffice

Record a Series of Actions and then Replay it Whenever Needed

When using LibreOffice, you can often find yourself repeating the same series of actions and wishing that there was a button that just did what you wanted in a single click. While LibreOffice can't possibly provide every combination of actions in a sensible way, it can give you the capability to do so yourself. LibreOffice does this by allowing you to create macros.

The term macro can be off-putting, as to some as it implies a need to know how to program. However, extremely powerful macros can be created that require no programming whatsoever. At its simplest, a macro is a recorded series of events that can be replayed at any point. A macro can range from inserting a simple piece of formatted text to something much more complicated as your recording can utilise many of LibreOffice's features.

The **Record Macro** option may be disabled by default as it is an experimental feature. To enable it, select **Tools** > **Options**, expand the **LibreOffice** subtree and select **General**. Then ensure that the **Enable experimental (unstable) features** checkbox is checked. For the best stability, it can be wise to enable the features before you record a macro and then disable them when you have finished.

To record and run a simple macro in Writer, just do the following:

1. Select **Tools** > **Macros** > **Record Macro**.

2. From this point everything you do will be recorded to be replayed later. You may try inserting a piece of text and applying some formatting.

3. When you have finished the actions that you wish to repeat. Select **Stop Recording** in the **Record Macro** dialog that will have appeared.

4. A dialog will pop-up and ask you to enter a name for your macro. You can also choose a location to place your macro, but the default location will probably be fine until you have created quite a few and you need to organise them.

5. You can now test your macro. Select **Tools** > **Macros** > **Run Macro...**

6. Open up the **My Macros** subtree and then the **Standard** subtree and select **Module1** so that your dialog appears similar to that shown below.

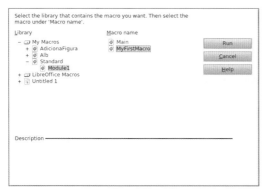

Running a macro

7. Select the macro that you have just recorded and then select **Run**.

You will now see the results of running the macro. If you were entering a piece of formatted text, then that text will be inserted into your document. Running the macro several times will insert the text several times.

Run Your Macros with a Single Click: Put them on the Toolbar

If you are running your macros through the **Run Macro** dialog you will soon notice that it can take quite a few clicks to bring up the dialog, find your macro, and then select **Run**. I'm sure that you'll feel that having to do this somewhat defeats the point of using a macro in the first place.

Fortunately, there is a much better way to run your macros – place them on the toolbar. LibreOffice enables you to insert your macros in its menus or on its toolbars. What's more it's easy to do and will save you a great deal of time.

To add one of your macros to a toolbar, simply do the following:

1. Select **Tools** > **Macros** > **Organize Macros** > **LibreOffice Basic...**

2. Select **Assign** in the **Basic Macros** dialog (don't worry about having to select the correct macro at this point).

3. Select the **Toolbars** tab in the **Customize** dialog.

4. The following screenshot shows this dialog. Here you can choose which toolbar you would like to insert your macro into. The default is the **Standard** toolbar which will usually be what you want.

Customise a toolbar

5. Select **Add…**

6. The **Add Commands** dialog will appear. Scroll to the bottom of the list and open up the **LibreOffice Macros** subtree and find the macro you wish to place on the toolbar. The dialog will now look similar to the following screenshot.

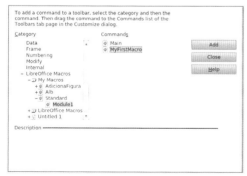

Add macro to toolbar

7. Select **Add** and then **Close**.

8. In the **Customize** dialog you will now see your macro in the list of commands on the toolbar.

9. Select **OK and then Close**. You will now see your macro appear in the standard toolbar.

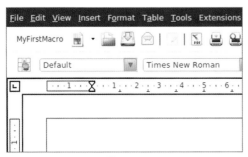

A macro on the toolbar

10. To run your macro, all you now need to do is click on the button in the toolbar.

 You can drag and drop your macro in the Customize dialog to control where it appears in the toolbar.

Use LibreOffice Basic to Create Involved Macros

Having said that macros do not require any programming skill does not mean that it is not possible to take advantage of those skills if you already possess them, or that it is not worth learning them if you don't. Languages such as LibreOffice Basic, Python and JavaScript are supported by LibreOffice internally. Other languages such as Java or C++ can use the application programming interface (API) to control LibreOffice. Of all these, LibreOffice Basic is probably the most common and the simplest.

As the name suggests, LibreOffice Basic has a lot in common with other Basic languages, such as VBA, and if you have experience with one of these you should find LibreOffice Basic relatively easy to pick up.

Create a New Module and a New Macro

Before you actually start any programming, the first step is to create a new macro and load it in the macro editor. This can be done with the following steps:

1. Select **Tools > Macros > Organize Macros > LibreOffice Basic**.

2. Expand the **My Macros** subtree and then select **Standard**.

3. Select **Organizer…**

4. The **Macro Organizer** will appear. Select **Standard** and select **New** to create a new module – a module can contain one or more macros, but for now the new module will have a single macro called **Main**.

5. Enter the name of your module, select **OK** and then select **Close** in the **Macro Organizer**.

6. You will now be back in the **LibreOffice Basic Macros** dialog. Select your new module in the tree and then select **Main** from the list on the right.

7. Select **Edit** to enable you to edit the script for this macro. The script editor is shown – as below – and you are now able to define behaviour for your new macro.

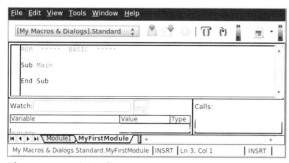

The macro script editor

Using LibreOffice Basic to Script a Macro

Unfortunately, there is not enough space in this book to provide a complete introduction to LibreOffice Basic. The following table describes some of the more useful keywords and then a small example puts them together to create a simple macro:

Keyword	Explanation
REM or '	Indicates that the text following is a *comment*. That is it has no function, it just provides useful information to the reader.
Dim	Declares a variable – an identifier for a value that may change.
Integer, Long, String	Defines the type of a variable. There are a wide range similar to those used in Base.
Const	Declares a constant – a value that always remains the same.
If, Then, Else, End If	Declares a conditional branch. If a value is true then do one thing, otherwise do the other.
For, Next	Declares a fixed iteration loop. Executes the enclosed loop a fixed number of times.
While, WEnd	Declares a variable loop. Executes the enclosed loop until a certain condition becomes true.
Sub, End Sub	Declares a procedure. The enclosed code can be executed by calling the procedure.

The examples below show how to use LibreOffice basic to count the number of paragraphs in a text document and then use a message box to display the result to the user.

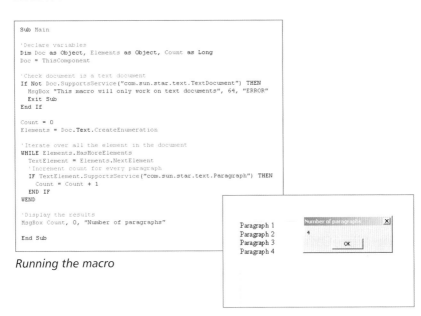

```
Sub Main

'Declare variables
Dim Doc as Object, Elements as Object, Count as Long
Doc = ThisComponent

'Check document is a text document
If Not Doc.SupportsService("com.sun.star.text.TextDocument") THEN
    MsgBox "This macro will only work on text documents", 64, "ERROR"
    Exit Sub
End If

Count = 0
Elements = Doc.Text.CreateEnumeration

'Iterate over all the element in the document
WHILE Elements.HasMoreElements
    TextElement = Elements.NextElement
    'Increment count for every paragraph
    IF TextElement.SupportsService("com.sun.star.text.Paragraph") THEN
        Count = Count + 1
    END IF
WEND

'Display the results
MsgBox Count, 0, "Number of paragraphs"

End Sub
```

Paragraph 1
Paragraph 2
Paragraph 3
Paragraph 4

Number of paragraphs
4
OK

Running the macro